You Can
Help Yourself

Jerry Schmidt

Harvest House Publishers
Irvine, California 92714

Dedication

To Karen, who creates an atmosphere of love, encouragement, and giving.

YOU CAN HELP YOURSELF
Copyright © 1978 Harvest House Publishers Irvine, California 92714
Library of Congress Catalog Number: 77-92734
ISBN # 0-89081-069-9

ACKNOWLEDGEMENTS

I wish to acknowledge several persons who have been inspiring and encouraging in my life. For one, Dr. Robert Embree, my advisor at Westmar College several years ago—he believed in me, when I didn't. Dr. Raymond Brock, Jim Collins, Wes Roberts, David Torbett, and H. Norman Wright have been helpful through the model of their lives. The constant encouragement of my wife, Karen, is also deeply felt. And, finally for models of giving and sacrificial love I acknowledge my parents, Art and Marvel Schmidt.

CONTENTS

1

You Can Help Yourself!

❧⸙❧

*"A person is constantly called upon to create his own
future.* —G. Baum

The young couple sat in front of me in my
counseling office. Expectantly, their eyes were
fixed in my direction, as if to say, "Dr. Schmidt,
we know you have the correct solutions to our
problems. We want you to change us and put
our lives back together." At the same time, other
thoughts go through their minds: "Soon you will
discover, Mr. Marriage Counselor, that all of
these problems are not my fault at all, but my
spouse's. He/She is the one who really needs to
change, not me.

When we are involved in a troubled
relationship, we usually believe that in order for
things to get better, the other person needs to
change, not us. While it may be true that there
are particular actions which others engage in
that just seem to trigger a negative response in
us, this feeling often comes from the attitude
that says, "I am not responsible for my own
behavior, or my own actions. God is, or my

spouse is, or it's all my parents' fault."

In the Old Testament, Ezekiel talks about the concept of *individual responsibility.* Instead of taking personal responsibility for what was happening to them, the people of his day were blaming their ancestors, parents, brothers, sisters, and spouses for their troubles. Ezekiel says, "not true!" in Chapter 18, verse 4, he very clearly warns them that each person is responsible for what they do. Again in verses 19 and 30 he repeats this principle: " 'What?' you ask. 'Doesn't the son pay for his father's sins!' No! For if the son does what is right he shall surely live . . . I will judge each of you . . . according to your own actions." (TLB)

Not only are we to be responsible for our own actions, we are instructed to first look at and change our own behavior before we attempt to help others change. In Matthew 7:3-5 Jesus says: "And why worry about a speck in the eye of a brother when you have a board in your own? Should you say, 'Friend, let me help you get that speck out of your eye,' when you can't even see because of the board in your own? Hypocrite! First get rid of the board. Then you can see to help your brother." (TLB) So much time is wasted blaming others for our problems! In my own family and in the families I counsel, getting past the finger-pointing blame game is critical. When each family member begins to ask the question, "What can I do differently that will help make my family life better," half of the struggle toward reconciliation and growth is accomplished.

Dr. William Glasser, has clearly supported

the principle that we are responsible for our own actions. He believes that people do not change unless they themselves make a commitment to change. More is accomplished by looking at our own behavior and working on changing it than by trying to get others to assume responsibility for us. [1]

The old blame game just doesn't work.

Thus we have three general principles for self-change:

1. Assume responsibility for your own actions.
2. Instead of pointing your finger at the other person's faults, examine your own behavior and develop a plan for self-change.
3. You must make the commitment to help yourself. No one else can make that value judgment that motivates you to change. Friends can suggest that you alter what you're doing. God can convict you to "turn around." But ultimately, only you can make the decision to grow.

Some of the most exciting changes I have witnessed in people's lives have come about when these three principles have been adhered to. I recently counseled with a young man named Bob who was very suspicious of everyone else's motives. He believed that the other persons around him were basically against him and that they were actively working to block his goals in life. If he failed at a job it was his boss' fault. Or else the job itself was beneath him or too boring for him to possibly succeed.

One day I asked him if he liked the way he was presently living. After a pause he looked at me with some puzzlement on his face and replied, "Well . . . no . . . I. . . I guess not." To which I further queried, "Do you want to go on living this way?" He was quiet for a moment and then blurted out, "Well, that's what you're here for, to change me." He had not answered my question and until he did later in the interview he was not willing to hear my next question, which was, "If you don't like the way you are presently living and you want to change, what can you do to change?" For until he had made the commitment to alter his own life patterns, nothing I could say or do would make any difference.

When Bob finally admitted that he was not happy with the way his life was going and that he really wanted to turn around, he began to do some beautiful things for himself. He answered my question "What can you do to change?" with the outline of a plan:

1. I will begin trusting people.
2. I love God and will seek his leadership every day through scripture and prayer.
3. I will make a list of my own goals.
4. I will write down steps that I can take to accomplish these goals.

My next question was "How are you going to put this plan into action?" After some discussion, Bob decided that he would write this basic plan on a note card. He would take time to remove the card from his pocket and read it through at breakfast, lunch and dinner every day of the week. This simple procedure reminded Bob what *he* had determined were his personal goals for the next several weeks. Notice that I was only asking him the right questions. *He* was supplying *his own* answers. In the following weeks we developed further answers to the "hows" of his action plan.

I didn't let Bob off the hook just yet. I had one more question. Psychologists are notorious for asking questions. I asked, "When are you going to put this plan into action?" He replied, "Oh, soon . . . soon." Then I pushed for even more certainty by suggesting, "How about today?" He grinned from ear to ear and admitted, "I see what you're getting at. You're right; if I'm serious about all of this . . . that I'm really unhappy with the way I've caused my life to be . . . then I'm the only one who can change that . . . and why put all of this off any longer? If I'm serious about making a turn around—and it's my number one priority—then why not start today?" I breathed a huge sigh of relief, sat back in my chair and answered, "With the help of God, begin . . . now!"

What Next

You may have noticed that in my discussion of Bob I developed some additional principles for self-change:

1. You must make a *value judgment* as to whether or not there are parts of your life which are unacceptable to you. Your boss can nag at you to change, friends can make a reasonable request for you to

modify a habit, or God can convict you through scripture and prayer. Yet, no one can force you to turn over a new leaf. Only you can! Ask yourself the question, "Am I happy with the way I am presently living?"

2. *If there are some nooks and crannies of your life that you are not satisfied with, do you want to change?* Not, do you want your spouse to change, or your employee, or your children. In Proverbs 28:13 we are reminded "A man who refuses to admit his mistakes can never be successful. But if he confesses and forsakes them he gets another chance." (TLB) In Psalms 101:2, David responds to prayers offered on his behalf at his coronation: "I will try to walk a blameless path, but how I need your help, especially in my own home, where I long to act as I should." (TLB) The King was, in effect saying, "I've got to clean up my own act before I can expect others to follow suit and live godly, decent lives. The point is, you must make the choice as to where you're going and what you will do during your short pilgrimage on earth.

3. *Assuming you wish to change some of your present behavior, what can you do to change? What can you do that would be better than what you are presently doing?* I Timothy 6:11 underlines this principle. Paul encourages Timothy, "Oh, Timothy, you are God's man. Run from all these evil

things and work *instead* at what is right and good, learning to trust him and love others, and to be patient and gentle." (TLB) Paul gave Timothy some advice about relating to people. Now Timothy had some food for thought. What could he do that would be better than exploiting people?
He could trust God to take care of him, have a loving attitude toward others, and practice patience and gentleness.

4. *Specifically, how will you put this new, more positive plan into action?* Bob initiated his action by writing what he proposed to do on a 3x5 note card. Timothy probably utilized his knowledge of God's word to translate Paul's words "love," "patient," and "gentle," into observable action. Some of these practices probably included visiting the sick and brokenhearted, listening to people's everyday problems, being patient with the immature but growing child and giving a gentle hug to a person in the midst of grief. To succeed, each needed a plan.

5. *When are you going to begin?* Where would the Christian Gospel be today if Christ had said, "Oh, I'll get started with my Father's business someday. No hurry, I've got lots of time. Maybe I'll begin next week after my vacation in Jerusalem." You know what happens in many families when a parent or spouse says, "Sure, I'll start thinking about bringing her flowers

or maybe I can take them all to the mountains for a picnic . . . but I just can't this week . . . got to get those reports out . . . I'll think about it next week for sure though." The question is: When are you going to do it? If it is a high priority, you're not satisfied with this particular area of your life, and you have set up an action plan for change, then why not begin?

The questions to ask are:

1. Do you like what you're doing and are you satisfied with this aspect of your life?
2. If you are dissatisfied, *what* can you do that would be better?
3. Specifically *how* will you go about acting out this new and better way?
4. When are you going to begin to act differently?

Let's walk through another example. A client of mine used this self-change process recently because she felt as though her relationships with her family members had disintegrated. In our conversations together, she acknowledged that she did *not like the way she was living*. It seemed that she was constantly in conflict with either her children or her husband. She could not understand why no one ever listened to *her*. Virginia felt as though she had lost the respect of her children. They kept telling her that she did not understand them, while Virginia was of the opinion that she knew exactly what they were thinking and feeling at all times. Virginia's husband, Bill, kept telling her that she never listened or even attempted to listen to what he was feeling.

Virginia approached her children and husband with the following statement: "I do not like the way things have been going in our family. We get into a lot of fights that I don't like and I'm sure you don't enjoy either. Tell me *what I could do better.*" Immediately she received the feedback "you could listen more to what we say." Thus, she now had the *what she could do that would be better*—listen!

The next question was, *how*? Here are several action steps that we worked out together. She listed them on a note card:

1. Whenever a member of my family says something to me I will look them straight in the eye and face that person squarely. If I cannot listen in this manner I will tell that family member that I can't listen to them at the moment and offer them an alternative time when I can.

2. I will spend at least five minutes per day listening attentively to each person in my family, without giving them advice or telling them what I think they *should* think or feel.

3. While I am listening to other people outside my family I will make good eye contact with them, lean forward, nod occasionally to encourage them to talk, and face them squarely.

4. At least twice per day I will summarize what I hear someone else saying to me,

until that person agrees that I've caught the gist of what they've said.

5. I will read the chapters on "Active Listening" in *Parent Effectiveness Training* by Thomas Gordon.

When was the final and toughest question to answer. Virginia had lots of reasons why she couldn't begin immediately. She didn't enjoy reading anything but novels, her husband would not be around much this week, what if her kids needed advice, etc? She finally agreed that if things were to get better (and she agreed that her situation was intolerable) inertia was not the answer. Thus, she decided to begin immediately. Very quickly, Virginia began to receive positive feedback, not only from family members, but from some of her co-workers as well.

The "When are you going to do it?" question is critical. If Virginia had continued her excuse-making, she would have successfully kept herself trapped in her own misery. The truth is, excuses are absolutely worthless. They only serve to keep you from action. Excuses attempt to put the blame for your dilemmas on everyone else. You can make a decision to change, now, without blaming yourself or anyone else, if you follow the steps *what, how* and *when.*

---

1. Wm. Glasser, *Reality Therapy* (Harper & Row, 1970).

2

Are You Satisfied With the Way Your Life Is Growing?

ו‿ד‿פ‿כ‿ים

"To grow is to change, and to have changed often is to have grown much."   —J.H. Newman

Let's take a deeper look at the initial question concerning self-change—"Are you satisfied with the way your life is growing?" To answer this question, you must have some goals for your life. In order to be committed to helping yourself grow as a person, you must select goals that you care about attaining. You are not going to be willing to expend much effort unless you are working toward something that really matters.

Throughout the pages of God's Word we read about Biblical characters who struggled with what was important for their lives—what goals to strive to reach. Jeremiah is one example. He felt that the Hebrew nation needed to be warned concerning their evil ways, and he felt called by God to do the warning. But he held back. He probably struggled with some of the same feelings and conflicts Jesus must have felt. As Charles Francis Potter, renown Bible scholar, states: "Both Jeremiah and Jesus were looked upon as heretics and destructive critics and charged with blasphemy and treason for predicting the destruction of the temple. In fact, when Jesus called it a den of thieves he was quoting Jeremiah." [1] Tradition says that Jeremiah once said, "Oh Lord, I cannot go as a prophet to Israel, for when lived there a prophet whom Israel did not desire to kill? Moses and Aaron they sought to stone with stones; Elijah the Tishbite they mocked at because his hair was grown long." Jeremiah was torn with indecision. On the one hand he felt called. He was compelled to act on that call. On the other hand he was fearful of the consequences of putting his beliefs on the line through action.

As we attempt to decide about what really matters in our lives we also experience that kind of struggle. On the one hand we prize our cherished values and ideals. Yet we fear the hard work involved in acting on our values. We fear that someone else will say that our new directions are silly or stupid. So we remain silent and inactive about what we feel is important. We tell ourselves that we ought not to have such a quick temper, or that we should really be more cheerful and optimistic. But we fail to act on these values because we have become so influenced by what others tell us that we begin to wonder if we have minds of our own. As Erma Bombeck suggests in the title of her book about life in the suburbs, *The Grass Is Always Greener Over the Septic Tank*. It's easier to believe that someone else has the answers, when in fact, we have answers in our own hearts about what is right for us. What we need to do is act on our values and then judge whether or not we're on the right track. As one of my colleagues recently said, "acting on commitments is the bread of life."

One result that I'd like for you to experience from reading this book is to make some decisions about what direction you want your life to be moving in and growing toward; and then for you to *act* on those decisions. Jesus acted on what he felt was important when he said "Let the children come unto me." Mary Magdalene acted on some values she cherished when she decided to follow Jesus. The Apostle Paul acted when he began *ministering* to Christians instead of slaughtering them.

What new directions, new beginnings do you have in mind for yourself? What values and ideals do you prize yet you continue to hesitate to act upon. *You* will have to take the initiative. As a fellow once said, "People who want milk should not seat themselves on a stool in the middle of a field in hopes that the cow will back up to them." David Campbell, a prominent psychologist states, "If you don't know where you're going, you'll probably end up somewhere else."[2] Where are *you* going?

Choosing What Really Matters

Take some time now to move toward answering the questions "Who am I?," "Whom do I wish to become?" and "What really matters to me?" The exercises that follow are designed to assist you in answering these questions. They have been used by persons who felt they needed some change in their lives, but were not very sure about *what* they wished to change. These strategies will help you identify some potential areas of self-improvement. They may point to the fact that you're off course with your life, or that you're not acting on the values which you cherish the most.

When you have finished the exercises you should have a clearer idea about your preferred direction for living. You will have, on paper, a basis for moving into the next chapter—"New Beginnings." Have fun with these activities. Share some of them with a friend or family member. Be sure you save what you have written for you'll need these materials in the next chapter.

Activity 1—Twenty Things I Love To Do

Take a sheet of paper and write the numbers 1 through 20 down the middle of the paper. Now think of things you most like to do. Big things or little things—it doesn't matter—as long as they are important to you. You might associate these 20 things with certain people, places, or seasons. Try to identify the situations, as they occur to you at random, by writing them to the right of the numbers you placed in the middle of the sheet. On the left side of the numbers, jot down certain information about the things you most like to do.

1. Write an M (for me) by those things you like to do alone. Write an O (for others) by the things you like to do with others. If you can go either way on a particular subject write down an M-O.

2. Put a $ by each activity that costs more than $5.00 each time you do it.

3. Most of us change our preferences frequently. Put the letters NP (for not previously) by those situations that would not have been important to you a few years ago.

4. Put an S by those things that tend to be spontaneous and a PA by those items you must plan ahead for. (For example, making reservations, calling someone in advance, buying tickets).

5. Out of the 20 things you like to do most, what five are the most important to you? Number those five in order of your preference.

6. Reviewing each of the 20 items, try to remember when you last did each item—jot down an actual or approximate date.

7. How often each year do you usually do each of these most favorite things? VO will mean very often, S will mean sometimes and HE will mean hardly ever.

8. Developing skills in any pursuit is a challenge. Indicate areas where you want to improve yourself with DS.

9. Many families pass along traits and skills. Look for things you would like to pass along. Code these PA.

10. Put the number 52 by those activities that you would want to do at least once each week for the rest of your life.

Finish the following sentences:[3]

I learned that I . . .

I was surprised that I . . .

I remembered . . .
I found it hard to believe . . .
I was saddened that I . . .
I enjoyed . . .
I never knew . . .
I plan to change . . .

Activity 2—Self Interview Exercises

Write a short paragraph answer to each of the following questions.

1. What are five activities that you would like to be doing five years from now?
2. If you had a million dollars tax free, what would you do with it?
3. If you were a Martian and had two weeks to spend on planet earth, what would you do during those two weeks? Be specific and account for your time in three hour blocks.
4. What makes you feel good?
5. Are there things about your family life that you would like to improve? If so, what are they?
6. If there was one thing you could change about yourself, what would it be?
7. What would you like to do more of in order to "get away from it all?"
8. What are you most afraid of?

Activity 3—Value Sorting

Rank the following values in the order of their greatest meaning to you: Asthetic, Loyalty, Power, Physical Appearance, Morality, Achievement, Knowledge, Justice, Recognition, Original-ity, Honesty, Religion, Wealth, Skill, Emotional Well-being, Pleasure, Altruism, Wisdom, Love, Autonomy, Health.

Now rearrange these same values in the order you feel has the greatest meaning to either society, your mother, your father, a friend, your school, or your boss. Finally, after comparing the lists write down your answers to the following:

1. Are you satisfied with your values? Which would you like to change?
2. Are your values similar to _____ (2nd list)? Is this a possible source of trouble or conflict? How?
3. Examine your top five or six values. Imagine the sort of life you will need to create in order to fulfill these values. Consider family, friends, recreation, occupation.

4. DECIDE—A step you are going to take this week to alter the rank of your values, resolve a conflict, or further your interests regarding family, friends, recreation, occupation—THE LIFE YOU WANT.

1. C.F. Potter. *The Great Religious Leaders*. (New York: Washington Square Press, 1962).
2. Donald Campbell. *If You Don't Know Where You're Going, You'll Probably End Up Somewhere Else*. (Niles, Illinois: Argus Communications, 1974).
3. Sidney Simon. *Meeting Yourself Halfway*. (Niles, Illinois: Argus Communications, 1974).

3

New Beginnings

"The flowers of all the tomorrows are in the seeds of today." —*Unknown*

What did you learn about yourself in the values exercises? Perhaps you were surprised by some of your responses. Did what you write bring to your awareness some ideas and feelings that you have suspected for some time? You may have even formulated the beginnings of a life goal or two, but that goal may still be rather vague and nebulous. For example, you may have said that you want to spend more quality time with a member of your family. Or perhaps you wish to enjoy your job more, lose weight, or spend more time in leisure activities. These are all worthwhile goals. However, if they remain in their present form, these intentions will hold little more power than the typical New Year's resolutions people make each January 1 and break by January 8. Some of your goals and discoveries may look something like this.

I wish I were less depressed.

I'd like to go camping more often.

I want to learn to control my temper.

I need more time for myself.

I want to be a better Christian.

I would like to travel more.

I need to learn how to listen to people.

I'm tired of being caught up in the constant battle of making money, getting ahead, keeping up with the Joneses.

I need to learn how to be more considerate.

I want to learn how to choose my own values as opposed to my mother's, father's, society's.

I want to enjoy myself more.

I'd like to be less lonely.

I'm such a nag. I'd like to change that.

I'm too hard on the kids. I yell at them too much.

I'd like to be more at ease with other people.

I wish I could express my opinion more often.

I'd like to switch jobs, but I'm scared to death that I wouldn't be able to find another position.

I'd like to become more active in my church.

How can you refine these goals and discoveries into more motivating, powerful statements which will lead to action? The answers will emerge as we explore the *what* and *how* questions discussed in the first chapter.

Pinpointing

The first step in beginning is *pinpointing*. Let

me explain. Pinpointing takes the guesswork out of goal setting. Pinpointing guides you toward self-change by allowing you to tell yourself specifically just what you intend to do. Let's say that your general goal is "to be kinder toward others." Sounds like a New Year's resolution, doesn't it? In its present form you have little chance of succeeding. Let's *pinpoint* some precise ways you can accomplish your general goal of "being kinder."

1. This week I will write a note to someone who has lost a loved person recently by death or divorce.
2. Each day I will say "Hi" to someone I pass on the way to work or school. This will be someone with whom I rarely speak. I will try to learn something new about at least one of these people during the week.
3. I will tell my wife that I love her, in some way, each day during this week. The "ways" will include such actions as saying "I love you," giving her a big hug, buying her favorite flower or perfume, preparing Saturday breakfast for the family, and telling her about some quality that I admire in her.
4. Thursday I will take my son fishing.

You can see that these goals are more precise and much clearer. You can much more readily judge whether or not you've taken your son fishing on Thursday than you can judge whether or not you've been kinder to people this week. Your snappy retort to this suggestion might be, "But I don't have the patience to change that slowly. Either I'm kind or I'm not. God wants me to change immediately. He's not satisfied with these small, insignificant alterations. I'm supposed to be a 'new person' in Christ."

Good point. But I believe that God delights in any small step that we take in the right direction. God's Word substantiates this: "The steps of good men are directed by the Lord. *He delights in each step they take.*" (Psalms 37:23 TLB) "Don't be impatient for the Lord to act! *Keep traveling steadily along his pathway* and in due season He will honor you with every blessing . . ." (Psalms 37:34 TLB) "You are living a brand new kind of life that is *continually learning more and more* of what is right, and *trying constantly* to be more and more like Christ who created this new life within you." (Colossians 3:10 TLB) These Scriptures tell me that growth and change do not come easily and quickly. They indicate that our Lord is pleased whenever we move along the pathway toward Christian maturity.

There is absolutely nothing wrong with setting small goals. They are more reachable and more realistic than large general goals. Psychological research indicates that an individual has a better chance of reaching goals that are stated in specific terms. Yet many of us mistakingly believe that we must change drastically and suddenly in order to feel good about ourselves. And when we fail to reach these unrealistic goals, we become disillusioned with ourselves because we have not changed overnight or because we have regressed to our usual behavior after only a few days. Just as it has taken time to learn our negative actions and attitudes it will take time, small steps, and hard work to learn better and more constructive behavior.

Accentuate the positive

Developing specific small steps is only part of the picture. Another ingredient is to increase positive things. Let's say that your goal is to be less of a nag around the people you care about. According to recent psychological principles it is far more effective to work on *increasing positive behaviors* than trying to *decrease negative actions*. Attempting to *decrease* the number of times you "nag" per day would not be as effective as working on *increasing* the number of positive remarks you say toward close friends or family members. Or your goal might be to become less depressed. Again, instead of trying to decrease your feelings of depression, it would be far more effective to work on doing things that excite you and make you feel good about yourself. Sally did just that. Here are some of her "small steps" for accentuating the positive:

1. Whenever I enter a room I will "scan my environment for positive things." That is, I will tune into such cues as a smile, a warm handshake, warm greetings, or any decorative item or furniture that I find attractive, etc.
2. I will allow myself at least 8 hours of sleep and/or rest per day.
3. I will eat 3 regular meals each day consisting of a well-balanced diet. (poor

eating habits can contribute to feelings of depression.)

4. I will spend some time each day with a close friend.

By continuing to concentrate on her feelings of depression, attempting to push them aside or chiding herself for feeling depressed, Sally would only increase her gloom. She needed to focus on actions which moved in the *opposite direction* of despondency. In one of Paul's letters to Timothy this principle of focusing on the positive is illustrated: "Oh Timothy, you are God's man. *Run from* all these evil things and *work instead* at what is right and good, learning to trust him and love others, and to be patient and gentle." (I Timothy 6:11 TLB)

There's another excellent reason for paying attention to ways you can increase the positives. If you were to decrease nagging or depression, and that alone, what would you replace these negative behaviors with? If you don't nag to get what you want anymore, how will you let people know what's going on with you? If you do nothing to replace nagging at this point, it is quite likely that some other negative response pattern—such as sulking—will creep in and you will have gained little in the way of positive growth. We do need to get rid of negative actions. But even more importantly, we need to replace these negatives with more positive steps that will serve the same function that the former negative response was fulfilling.

Difficulty of the goal

You can identify a goal that is important to

you, make it precise, and state it in positive terms and still have an unattainable goal. How? By setting your sights too high. For example, one person wanted to become more conversational. He set as his goal: "I will speak up in class at least five times each day." Now this ambition was stated in specific terms. It was stated positively. But the person who set it found himself having difficulty even getting off the ground. He went through an entire week and managed to tally only one comment in class for the entire week. He gave up the entire project in quiet resignation. What had gone wrong? He had set an unreasonably high goal. How could he have avoided this? He could have taken a count of how many times per day he was presently speaking up in class. If he had done this he probably would have discovered that he only spoke up about once a week. With that kind of data, it would have been more realistic to begin with a goal just above his present performance. For example, his goal might be to speak up at least three times *per week*. You can easily see that he would have greatly increased his chances of succeeding and of continuing the project.

If you are setting goals for yourself, a good place to begin is with an estimate of how often your pinpointed action presently occurs. Or you could actually count how often it is presently happening. Then begin by setting a goal that is just above your present average. Once you have reached your goal, set a new, slightly more difficult one. Present research indicates that by taking small gradual steps toward the ultimate goal you will greatly increase your chances of self-improvement.[1] Thus, if you are wanting to "take more short vacation trips" this summer, look first at how many you went on *last* summer and then increase your trips by a realistic amount. Or if you would like to be able to express your opinion more often, take a couple of days to count how often you are presently doing this. Then set your goal at one or two more of such comments per day. Once you have reached your goal, increase it by one or two per day. If you'll be patient, you'll get there!

Getting Started

It's time for some practice in pinpointing goals. For each of the general goals listed below, I have developed some "small beginnings." These little steps represent small, specific acts that together help to accomplish the general goal. I have also left a few blank spaces so that you can add more "steps" to the list. Fill in as many of the blanks as you can. Remember, make them precise and positive. The practice will help you pinpoint some things you want to change.

Goal:
I'd like to go camping more often.

Small Beginnings:
1. I will collect brochures on camping sites from my state from the Chamber of of Commerce by Wednesday of this week.

2. I will buy a new tire for the right wheel of the camper trailer by Thursday of this week.

3. I will enlist the help of my family to help me clean up the inside of our camper. My goal is to finish this task by Saturday noon.

4. Before the end of the week I will plan two camping trips with our family. This will include a decision about the camp sites, days we will camp and routes that we will travel to get to the sites.

5. (You add one)

_____

_____

_____

6. (One more, please)

_____

_____

_____

Now look at the "small beginnings" you wrote. Are they specific? Would I be able to judge from your description whether or not you actually reached your goals? Are they stated positively? Let's try another one.

Goal:

I want to be a better Christian.

Small Beginnings:

1. I will spend five minutes per day in silent prayer and meditation.

2. I will pray audibly in the presence of other family members at least every other day.

3. I will volunteer for one church activity where I feel I am contributing to my own Christian growth.

4. I will introduce myself to at least one visitor who is new to our church, during the coffee hour on Sunday morning.

5. (You add one)

_____
_____
_____

6. (Another one, please)

_____
_____
_____

Goal:
I need to learn how to be more considerate.

Small Beginnings:
1. I will read the following verse at the beginning of each day: "Life is short and we have never too much time for gladdening the hearts of those who are traveling the dark journey with us. Oh, be swift to love, make haste to be kind!"—Amiel
2. Each week I'll do a job around the house that everyone else hates to do. I'll do it as my gift to the other family members.
3. I will express a positive feeling that I have toward someone at work at least three times this week.
4. **I will take a friend to lunch this week.**
5. (You add one)

_____
_____
_____

6. (Another one, please)

_____

_____

_____

7. (One more)
_____

Goal:
I would like to be able to speak up more in a group.

Small Beginnings:
1. Each time I am in a group, I will ask at least one question of the person I feel closest to in the group.
2. At least once during each of the next three Church School sessions I will say out loud "I agree" to a statement someone else makes.
3. I will express a personal opinion at least once during the next neighborhood party.
4. (You add one)

_____

_____

_____

5. (Another)

_____

_____

_____

Let's review the important principles of goal setting:
1. Identify goals that are significant to you.
2. Write your goals down.
3. Pinpoint your goals by:
   • making them specific
   • stating them positively

- attaching numbers to them, when possible
- taking small, realistic steps toward your general goal

Go back now and check to see if your responses to the above exercises reflect these principles. If they do, you're ready to develop some of your own goals and initiate some of your own beginnings. If you've missed a principle or two, restate those responses that appear to be in error. Then begin to develop some of your goals. In order to increase the chances that you will follow through, write your "small steps" on a note card and carry the card with you. Take the note card out several times each day and read it. This will give you that gentle nudge you need to act!

But What If You Fail?

Let's say that you set what you think is a reasonable goal. You attempt to accomplish it and you fail to reach the goal. Does the world have to come crashing down around you? No! Again, I'd like to remind you of David's words in the Psalms: "The steps of good men are directed by the Lord. He delights in each step they take. *If they fall it isn't fatal, for the Lord holds them with his hand.* (Psalms 37:23, 24 TLB) And remember the words of Paul? " . . . forgetting what lies behind and straining forward to what lies ahead, I press on . . ." (Phil. 3:13-14 RSV) God did not intend for us to dwell on our mistakes or failures. As I read any one of the Gospels, I do not get the impression that Jesus spent more time stating what people could do that would be better, then telling them what they had done wrong.

In an interesting book entitled, *Personal, Balanced Goal Development*, Dr. John R. Van de Water describes what I call the "guided missile principle." Van de Water states that the guided missile is seldom on target, when it takes off the launch pad. In fact, it has to adjust itself a number of times. He says:

> "And suppose when it got its first input, this guided missile said to itself, 'Oh! I made a mistake! I'm terrible! I must be humble about this. I'll probably keep on making mistakes!! If it said that to itself, what would happen, the next time it got an input? It would feel bad and veer off in the wrong direction, wouldn't it? Because it would have programmed making mistakes. That reaction to a mistake is restrictive thinking and it leads to atrophy. But what a mistake is meant to do, is to lead to corrective thinking and to growth. The guided missile has been programmed by the scientist to think the way we're supposed to think. In its case, it doesn't even cross its mind, it 'made a mistake.' All it says to itself, is: 'next time, I'll go that way!' And it adjusts. And then it gets a new input, and it's off, the opposite direction; and it says to itself: 'Next time, I'll go that way.' And it uses error to correct itself toward perfection. So the men at Jet Propulsion Laboratory and Hughes Aircraft tell us, they landed Surveyor I, 36 feet from the pinpoint, 13

seconds late, on the moon! Now that's what you call quite a change arising, because of **an attitude change.**" [2]

God didn't design us as computers, thank goodness. But we were also not designed to focus on our mistakes. Instead we are to "press on," "take that next step," and focus on "what can I do that would be better." Set what you think is a realistic goal and try to accomplish it. If you don't reach that goal, you've lost nothing. Simply revise your goal. Perhaps there is a step that you need to take before you can accomplish the more ambitious goal you set originally. The important thing is to not put yourself down for missing the mark. Instead, stop and break your goal down into smaller steps to maximize your chances for progress.

Planting your own flower garden

Look again at your exercises from Chapter 1. Pick out one goal that these exercises suggest is important to you. Pinpoint five steps or "beginnings" that you could do that would move you toward your more generally stated goal. Check to see if your little steps are specific, observable, positive, realistic, and significant. Perhaps you'll want to sequence these steps so that, for example, Step 1 must be done before **you can move on to Step 2. Then write your goals** on a note card and carry it with you. Read the card several times each day.

When are you going to begin?

1. M.J. Mahoney and C.E. Thoresen. *Self-Control: Power to the Person.* (Monterey, California: Brooks/Cole, 1974).
2. John R. Van de Water. *Personal, Balanced Goal Development.* (Hawthorne, California: Promanent International, 1972).

4

Speaking the Truth in Love
Part I

"If only I may grow—firmer, simpler, quieter, warmer"
—*D. Hammerskjold*

Do you feel that people do not understand what you need or want from them? Do you find yourself avoiding disagreements at all costs? Are most of your days filled with disappointments, criticism and failures? What happens when someone gives you a compliment; do you deny the compliment? Would you like to make friends, but find it difficult to take the first step in doing so? Is it difficult for you to say "No" to a request when you'd really rather not do what was asked of you? Do you find it difficult to talk about yourself in a positive way?

If you found yourself nodding your head in the affirmative to some or most of these questions, these next two chapters are very important for you.

AGGRESSIVE, ASSERTIVE, PASSIVE

There are three general types of human behavior: aggressive behavior, assertive behavior and passive behavior. Those of you who were answering, "yes" to some or most of the above questions, were expressing either an aggressive or a passive manner of behavior.

Aggressive Behavior

What do I mean by aggressive? Let's say that you want a member of your family to clean the garage and you say, "I suppose it would be too much to ask your excellence to even put your finger on the broom and push it around the garage." That's an example of aggressive behavior. In making a request in this manner, you would be stepping on the other person's toes, ignoring his dignity and failing to take that person's feelings into consideration. This way of communicating would also successfully alienate the other person. Instead of using his hands to push the broom around, this person would probably like to place them tightly around your neck and squeeze!

All too often we fail to recognize that put-downs, name-calling, sarcasm, and coercion are only successful in alienating us from others. Part of the problem is that we recognize this fact only after the damage has been done and we've already blasted away. Scripture speaks of the power of our words: "But no one can tame the tongue; it is a restless evil and full of deadly poison. With it we bless our Lord and Father; and with it we curse men, who have been made in the likeness of God; from the same mouth come both blessing and cursing. My brethren, these things ought not to be this way" (James 3: 8-10 NASB). "Death and life are in the power of the tongue . . . Proverbs 18:21 NASB). "How long will you torment me, and crush me with words? (Job 19:2 NASB)."

Adding to the dilemma is the fact that aggressive behavior is often rewarded. For example, the boss who screams at her secretary, "You'd better get this letter out today or else!" will probably see the finished letter on her desk, ready for signing within seconds! Thus, the secretary's quick response has rewarded the boss for stomping all over her secretary. Or consider the father who constantly forces his children to do whatever he wants them to do, seldom taking their feelings or opinions into account. He will probably be regarded *initially* for his aggressive, non-caring actions through his children's fearful compliance. But watch out later when his children become older and the father is no longer able to physically restrain them. At that time they will rebel, either openly or quietly and surreptitiously. Paul, writing to the Christians at Ephesus, warns: "And now a word to you parents. Don't keep on scolding and nagging your children, making them angry and resentful. Rather, bring them up with the loving discipline the Lord himself approves, with suggestions and godly advice" (Ephesians 6:4 TLB). One thing we know for certain from psychological research and from every indication in the Scriptures is that aggressive behavior tends to arouse anger, vengeance and hostility in the person being attacked. Another certainty is that although aggressive actions on our part may initially bring compliance, the end result will usually be alienation and loneliness.

Passive Behavior

Passive behavior is the exact opposite of aggression. Passive people tend to be doormats, allowing others to walk all over them. They seldom let people know what they want or think and are usually unable to say "no" and stick to it. Passive people also have difficulty making friends and may find it utterly impossible to accept or give a compliment. They usually avoid disagreements at all cost, saying to themselves, "He might be unhappy if I disagreed with him."

If you find yourself doing and thinking some of the following, then portions of your everyday actions are passive and self-defeating:

1. Constantly saying to yourself things like, "She'll be disappointed if I don't do what she wants."
2. Concerned about meeting the expectations of everybody else first, no matter how much you are in need.
3. Simple decisions become difficult because you want to please everyone.
4. Constantly wish you could do certain things, yet never getting to actually do them.
5. Thinking, "They'll believe I'm conceited if I say something nice about myself."
6. Wanting to meet someone, but hesitating

to do so out of fear they will reject you.

7. Being very indirect in your conversation with others.
8. Collecting a lot of anger, because you haven't spoken up on a daily basis concerning your own feelings.
9. Attempting to read the other person's mind to make sure you are always saying what they want to hear.
10. Consistently feeling as though you have to be submissive in order to keep peace.

Assertive Behavior

Christians are told to grow up "speaking the truth in love" (Ephesians 4:15 NASB). Ephesians 4:25 says, "Therefore, rejecting all falsity and done now with it, let everyone express the truth with his neighbor, for we are all parts of one body and members one of another" (Amplified). Looking through a large number of the recent books on assertiveness, I could not find a better definition of the term: Assertive people communicate honestly. They are positive in their relations with others, and take responsibility for themselves. Such persons stand up for their own rights without ignoring the rights of others. The best example we have of the assertive life is that of Jesus. He spoke his mind with his disciples in the Garden of Gethsemane when they fell asleep during the time he needed them most. Jesus was so full of agony that "his sweat became like great drops of blood" falling down upon the ground. Returning to his closest friends, he found them asleep and said to them, "Why do you sleep? Rise and pray that you may not enter into temptation." (Luke 22:46 RSV). Jesus experienced a human need. He needed the concern and prayers of his friends. And he expressed his need openly and directly.

With the Pharisees, Jesus was direct and assertive. He answered their questions with honesty and candor. (For a good example, read Luke 20 in the Living or Amplified Bibles.) There are countless other examples of Christ's assertiveness. Passing the sycamore tree which Zacchaeus had climbed into, "Jesus looked up at Zacchaeus and called him by name! 'Zacchaeus!' he said, 'Quick! Come down! For I am going to be a guest in your home today!'" (Luke 19:5 TLB).

When Jesus called out to Peter, James and John to follow him and become his disciples, he did not say, "Come on you unfortunate slobs, consider yourselves lucky to follow such a hotshot like me." That would have been an aggressive response, the kind of response that I've heard in other forms in today's business world. He did not coax them to follow him by beating around the bush. Can you imagine him saying, "Do you think that you might be able to . . . er . . . that is . . . you probably wouldn't consider following me for just a few hours and try to sort of . . . follow me." No, Jesus was not a passive person. He was direct, yet not abusive. He took the guesswork out of communication by stating straightforwardly, "Come, follow me!" (Mark 1:17 TLB). You see, Christ believed that people were responsible for themselves and could make their own decisions about what they would and would not do. So why beat around the bush and waste time and energy with indirect, deceitful approaches. He would ask men to be his followers in an honest, positive manner. If they refused that was their choice. And if they accepted, they knew exactly what they were saying "yes" to.

Assertiveness is Situational

One final word about assertiveness as a principle for living. *It may not always be possible to be assertive.* For instance, you want to say something directly to your boss, but, based upon experience you know that you could lose your job in the process. You have made the decision to keep your job. In that case, knowing the consequences you might choose not to be assertive. That's okay, because, you are still being responsible for your own behavior. You, ultimately, have to live with the consequences.

ASSERTIVE BEHAVIORS

In an interesting and helpful book, *Project You*[1], written by Claudine Paris and Bill Casey, ten types of assertive behaviors are discussed. In this chapter and the next, I want to list some of these behaviors and give you examples and offer strategies for becoming more assertive in your own life.

Think and Talk About Yourself In a Positive Way

Some people spend a lifetime waiting for others to notice the good things they do. I have counseled with many of these individuals and find they have become totally bitter about life and people in general. These people make statements like, "nobody appreciates me, my boss never notices the good things I do, my family could care less whether I live or die." Joshua Liebman in *Peace of Mind* said, "He who hates himself, who does not have a proper regard for his own capacities . . . can have no respect for others; deep within himself he will hate his brothers when he sees in them his own marred image."[2] Now it may be true that you have a non-complimentary boss or that your family frequently takes you for granted. Yet there is also some real truth in the adage "charity and love begin with yourself."

Let me give an example of this adage at work. My five year old son, Cory, observes very carefully what Mommy and Daddy do and say. And like any other imperfect parents, we occasionally model some pretty erroneous behavior. However, recently it became obvious to us that we do model for Cory how to "talk about yourself in a positive way." One morning he came to the breakfast table all aglow. I was sleepily munching on some cornflakes when he blurted, "Daddy, guess what . . .I washed my hands last night before dinner . . . I ate all my dinner . . . and I even washed my hands before breakfast this morning . . . what do you think of that?" I could have said, "Cory, shame on you . . . you mustn't brag like that . . . the Bible says that we should be humble." But thank God I did not! Note that Cory was not being boastful or competitive. He did not say, "Look Daddy, I have much cleaner hands than Ryan" (our younger son) or "I eat a lot better than Jennifer" (one of his friends). He was merely proud of his own ability to follow through on some actions that we knew were important to us, and he felt good about doing them. If he would not have mentioned the fact that he had clean hands and had eaten well the evening before, I would not have noticed and Cory would not have received my genuinely positive response. Cory had seen Karen and I talk about ourselves in a postive way often enough that he also had the courage to speak up and tell us about his own success. That kind of action builds self-esteem.

I have been a professor at a major University for the past five years and one of the things I have done is to keep my boss aware of the positive endeavors I'm involved in. Each time I have written a major publication, given a workshop, been asked to speak for a group or developed some new ideas for a class I have either mentioned these activities to him or written him a short note explaining what I've done. How else would he know what kind of growth I'm involved in? How else could he be aware of the extent of my motivation to do a good job? My alternative would have been to sit around and wait for him to find out about what I'm doing and then become resentful when he did not happen to receive a vision that I had done something which I was proud of.

I am not saying that we should all become braggarts, comparing ourselves with others, like the self-righteous Pharisee who prayed, "Thank God, I am not a sinner like everyone else,

especially like that tax collector over there."
(Luke 18: 11 TLB).

What I am saying is that it's okay to like yourself. It's okay for you to share the spotlight with others. It's okay to be proud and pleased with something you've done. Love yourself. God doesn't make junk!

Small Beginnings

Here are some ways you can begin thinking and talking about yourself positively:

1. As often as you can today, say to yourself "That's neat," or "Good for me" or "Praise God," whenever you say, think or do something which you regard as positive. Perhaps you've complimented one of your children for something you usually overlook. Or you remembered to have devotions. Give yourself credit. Compliment yourself!

2. Say something positive about yourself to someone you don't know very well. For example, "I finished my reports today!" Or "I got together with a friend today."

3. Think of five things you like about yourself.

4. Write a letter to someone in which you state something positive about yourself.

5. Call someone on the phone. During the conversation say something positive about yourself.

6. Tell someone about a situation you handled well.

Now you add some of your own small beginnings that relate to this assertive behavior:

7. _____

8. _____

9. _____

Express Honest Compliments

God's Word tells us to "encourage one another" (I Thess. 5:14). Research psychologists tell us that there is nothing that can motivate people more than positive feedback. They refer to "positive strokes," "encouragement," "positive reinforcement, and "positive thinking." If you appreciate someone or something they did, tell them. Let people know that you value even the thing they "should" do like: cooking meals, doing schoolwork, shoveling the snow from the walk, buying groceries, typing a letter or finishing a job on schedule.

Compliments should be sincere and specific. If the only motive you have in mind for your kind words is flattery, forget it. People can see right through your insincerity. The positive feedback you're giving must be true. Second, your compliments should be specific. Instead of saying to a child, "You're a good mathematician!" it would generally be better to describe what you see that is good and what you're pleased about. For example, "You did your math problems and they're all correct; that's neat!" Now, those are words a budding young third grader can believe, especially if he has been struggling with math concepts all year. Below are listed some general compliments, along with some more specific ways of saying them:

General: "You're a super lover."
Specific: "I like the way you rub my neck."

General: "You're fantastic."
Specific: "I like the way you express yourself."

General: "You're a great receptionist!"
Specific: "I like the way you put people at ease."

In my own family counseling practice I have noticed time after time how the wife complains that her husband does not give her specific reasons why he loves her. Men, if you want to really build some warmth between you and your wife, give her some *sincere, specific* compliments. Of course, that works both ways. Wives, should feel perfectly free to do the same!

If you have difficulty expressing your appreciation toward others, begin with non-verbal compliments. For example, *eye contact* alone is a compliment to someone with whom you are speaking. Looking directly into the speaker's eyes says to that person that you value them and what is being said. And this is certainly a compliment. *Winking* at someone is another type of non-verbal positive feedback. *Nodding* or *smiling* are still other forms of simple, low risk compliments.

Since positive feedback is the most powerful human motivator, employers who are sick and tired of reminding, cajoling or yelling at people to do their work, might try giving positive feedback to employees who are doing their work. Or, if your are in a troubled relationship at home and are weary of the constant fighting and bickering, begin today giving one honest, specific compliment per day to that significant other person. Then increase that number to two per day . . . three . . . four and watch what happens.

In general, accentuating the positive does several things:

1.   It helps you develop into a positive, fun person to be around.
2.   It helps you discover more of the positive aspects of life and decreases the chance that you will become caught up in a bitter kind of existence.
3.   You become a model of kindness toward others at work, home, church, etc. (Incidentally, God's Word refers to the word, kind, about 150 times!)

I'd like to ask you two simple thought questions:

1.   *Are you kinder to the people in your own family or to strangers?* John Gottman, in a significant book on couple communication, has stated: "The most consistent research finding about what is different in the communication of strangers and people married to each other is that married people are ruder to each other than they are to strangers. They interrupt their spouses more, put their spouses down

more, and are less complimentary to each other."[3]

2. *When was the last time that you actually scanned your environment for positive things? When was the last day that you looked more for positive happenings than you did for the negative?*

Small Beginnings

Here are some small beginnings toward expressing honest compliments:

1. Smile at someone you don't know.
2. Give eye contact and smile at someone you care for.
3. Compliment someone for a specific behavior ("I like the way you listen to me.").
4. Touch someone and smile.
5. Tell someone you appreciate their love, friendship, help, or support.
6. Thank someone for doing something they were "supposed to do."
7. Set a goal to give a certain number of compliments per day.

Now add your own small beginnings. What are you willing to do this next week.?

8. _____

9. _____

10. _____

Accept Compliments

I'm appalled by the number of people I see in counseling who give compliments back instead of acknowledging and accepting them. I am convinced that denying compliments is a leading single cause of low self-esteem in our society. Not accepting a compliment that someone gives you is the epitomy of conceit. What we are saying when we deny someone else's positive feedback is that we know better than they do, and that they have really poor judgment.

What do I mean by giving a compliment back? Let's say that someone compliments you on your attire. You reply, "Well, it really isn't very stylish, not ironed too well; I just grabbed it out of the closet this morning in the dark." What you are really saying to that person is, "I don't deserve the compliment . . . you don't have very good judgment . . .I can't handle compliments, so don't give me any more . . . give me negative feedback, I can handle that!" Do that often enough and that person will probably not disappoint you.

Often, one of our own self-thoughts gets in the way of accepting an honest compliment from someone: "I don't deserve it." But what does God's Word say about this thought? Luke 7:28 states that God values each person highly. Romans 5:8 says God loved us even as sinners. And Ephesians 3:11-12 assures us that we can have boldness and confidence in Christ.

So what can we do that would be better than telling people around us that we don't deserve positive feedback? We can look that person straight in the eye, smile and reply, "Thank you." It's as simple as that! We can say, "Thanks for the feedback," "I appreciate that," or "Thanks for the compliment." In this way we are doing a couple of important things. One, we are encouraging others to give us positive feedback. By saying "thank you" we are in effect saying "you have good judgment" . . . "I enjoy positive feedback" . . . "You can do that again!" And they probably will! Two, we increase the chances of our developing positive self-esteem. If we increase honest, direct, positive nourishment, we also raise the probability of feeling good about ourselves. And what can be wrong with that? One of the foremost causes of troubled relationships that I see at home, work, parties, or church is low self-esteem. And one thing you can do immediately to raise your own self-esteem is to accept compliments. Begin, today!

1. Claudine Paris and Bill Casey, *Project You* (Denver: Institute of Living Skills, 1976).
2. Joshua Liebman, *Peace of Mind* (New York: Simon & Schuster, 1946), p. 71.
3. John Gottman, *A Couple's Guide to Communication* (Champaign, Illinois: Research Press, 1976), p. 45.

5

Speaking the Truth in Love
Part II

*"If I am not for myself, who will be for me? But if I am
for myself alone, what am I?"*   —*Talmudic Saying*

The last chapter considered some of the lower
risk, easier assertive actions we can practice
and learn. This chapter will deal with some of
the more risky ideas. But don't be faint of heart,
growth usually involves some sort of risk. So,
let's begin!

Ask For What You Want

Have you ever experienced this scene? It's
Saturday night. Perhaps you are with a friend or
sweetheart. You're both thinking about what
you could do together for the evening. Your
friend is thinking about attending a party, while
you are wanting to go to a movie. But neither of
you speak up for what you want. Instead, the
first audible sound comes from your friend,
"Well, what do you want to do?" "Oh, I don't
know. What do you want to do?" you reply. Your
friend mumbles something about a party that
you know you don't want to go to. You mumble
something about a movie but quickly add that

you can probably go next week. As a result, you both end up aimlessly drifting off to the party. The result is that you end up having a miserable evening, and become very angry with your friend who has "forced you to attend the party." You've both just lost a game of "I don't know, what do you want?"

Recently, I counseled with a couple on their marriage relationship. The husband, Steve, rarely asked his wife, Susan, for what he needed or wanted in their relationship. He would call from work and say vague things like "I just don't know what I'm going to do about this job." What he really needed from Susan was for her to just listen to his quandry at work for a moment and support him in whatever decision he came up with. Yet he never came right out and asked, "I just need for you to listen to me for a few minutes."

Susan rarely knew what Steve really wanted in their relationship. As a result, Steve became more convinced that Susan just did not care about his needs. His silence and vagueness coupled with Susan's resulting non-response led to Steve's suicide attempt and his threats to leave home. As Steve was furiously moving his clothes and personal belongings out of the house, he finally blurted out, "It would only take three words to keep me here; those words are 'I love you.'" That was the first direct request Steve had made of Susan in 10 years of marriage and after Susan recovered from the shock she responded very quickly and directly with those three words Steve had asked for! Each time I think of this situation I can't help but see both the humor and the tragedy. Steve had gone through 10 years of agony, largely because he did not ask for what he wanted. And when he saw the willingness of Susan to respond to his requests, he was absolutely floored.

Asking for what you want does not guarantee that you'll always get it. To expect that would be to act like a child who "wants what he wants" and "wants it now!" The point is that unless you make your needs known to other people, how else will they discover what you want? Try as we might, man has yet to come up with a good technique for mind reading. Yet a lot of wasted time and energy is spent trying to read each other's minds in business relationships, personal interactions and with day to day acquaintances.

What happens when people do not express their needs to each other openly? One major pattern I see is the build-up of anger and self-pity. If you or I go around expecting other people to read our mind, then the next step is to begin saying to ourselves, "she just doesn't care what I think" . . . "he never does anything I want" . . . "he should know what I'm thinking or wanting" . . . "why should I have to tell her?" At some point, our bitterness blows up in someone's face as we present them with a whole list of injustices. The other person is initially quite shocked and confused about our feelings because they had no idea we were thinking these things! The self-pity we talk ourselves into here creates within us an attitude that we are not responsible for ourselves. Others are. And as we discovered in chapter one, this idea is simply false.

As mentioned before, Jesus certainly asked for what he wanted. In Luke 19:28-35 Jesus sends two of his disciples to Jerusalem to find a donkey. "Untie him," Jesus said, "and bring him here." Moses, also, appeared to be an assertive person, not afraid to ask for what his Lord wanted. Imagine standing in front of Pharaoh, the head of the "White House" of his day, demanding that he " Let my people go!" These Biblical models of Christian behavior are a far cry from the martyred spouse who stomps down the basement stairs emitting groans and grunts audible over the entire neighborhood, in order to hint that he or she needs help cleaning the basement. Moses would have simply stated, "I need your help to clean the basement." Don't hint. Ask for what you want in a straight-forward, loving manner.

Small Beginnings

Again, here are some suggestions for getting started with asking for what you want.

1. Ask for an opinion.
2. Ask for a clarification of what someone says.
3. Ask for a favor.
4. Ask for a behavior change (e.g. "Could you please speak more loudly?")
5. Begin your sentences with phrases such as "Would you please . . ."
   "I would appreciate you saying . . ."
   "I need . . ."

Some Points to remember:

1. People have the right to refuse your requests.

2. Requests are not demands! You can't *make* a person do anything unless you use physical force.

3. Make your requests in a direct, loving manner.

4. Do not ask for what you want when you are extremely angry. Wait until you've cooled down.

State Honest Disagreements With Ease

Stating disagreements "with ease" is tough for most of us. Let's take a look at how we can approach this goal.

If you are a human being with values of your own you will discover times when you disagree with what other people have to say. Sometimes you will choose to remain silent, but other times you will want to speak out for the values you hold, especially if your silence could be interpreted as compliance or agreement with an opinion that is completely contrary to what you hold as sacred.

Can you imagine what this world would be like if no one had ever openly disagreed with anyone else? Christianity would never have been founded; the United States would not be a reality; and instead of hopping aboard a jetliner to Calgary, Canada next month I'd be walking, starting last January.

In disagreeing with someone else we often have the thought that "perhaps they won't like

me anymore, and I don't want that to happen."
What this attitude fails to consider is that we
could be increasing the risk of that person not
liking or respecting us because we *do not* speak
up for what we believe in. I see children and
adolescents who simply do not respect their
parents because Mom and Dad seldom, if ever,
state their opinions directly. Children des-
perately need for parents to share their own
values, philosophies and opinions about life. Our
little ones must have adult models so they can
have a basis and "home ground" to begin living
their own life. Certainly there comes a time
when they will choose their own values and
ideas, but they cannot do a very good job of this
in the vacuum of permissiveness. We need to
share our values with our kids and act on them,
so they can see what "believing in God" or
"trusting each other" looks like.

Some Principles for Disagreeing

Here are some guidelines to consider when
you choose to openly disagree with someone:

1. *Stick to the issue*
   Many disagreements develop into all out
   battles because of "kitchen sinking."
   These people drag everything into the
   conversation except the kitchen sink. The
   discussion starts on one issue and before
   there is a chance to explore that issue,
   one person or the other drags in other
   disagreements that usually are not even
   related. When "kitchen sinking" occurs,
   a simple "I think we're getting off track"

may be all that is needed.

2. *Don't attack the other person.*

   Many problems arise when we stop talking about the issue and begin to attack the other person. If you have difficulty with this, write down the following two verses on a note card, carry the card around with you, and read it several times a day:

   > "Self-control means controlling the tongue! A quick retort can ruin everything." Proverbs 13:3 TLB

   > "A good man thinks before he speaks; the evil man pours out his evil words without a thought." Proverbs 15:28 TLB

3. *Disagree first on small matters in low risk relationships.*

   By doing this you'll get a feel for what it's like for you to disagree with someone. You'll also discover the kind of tactics people use to get you off the track. For example, at a social gathering a few days ago, I was seated next to a person from out of state. He immediately began complaining about the rotten weather we were having in our city, how smoggy it was and how unfriendly the people were. This was a person I would probably never again see. Thus he represented a low risk relationship. He continued, "This city is cold, smoggy and unfriendly. There is no way I'd live here." I responded by saying "I don't know what cities you've been in.

I've really experienced my city as having a comfortable, moderate climate with lots of warm, sunny days." He added, "Well the people here are really cold and ruthless." I replied, "My experience has been different than yours on that score also. I've had more close friends here than in any other community I've lived."

When I disagreed I did not criticize him for his attitude. I stated my opinion and the specific reasons I had for forming my opinion. I did not attempt to reform him. I merely asserted my point of view. This illustrates two more principles:

4. State your opinion and the specific reasons for forming your opinion.
5. Do not attempt to reform the other person.

Once you are able to disagree about small unimportant matters in low risk relationships, move on to issues of greater importance for you. Some of these "heavier" topics could be which pro team will win the division title, how to raise children, politics, religion, the future of the American family, or women's liberation.

The next step is to speak out about unimportant issues with persons you know more intimately. Finally, you can ease into important issues with those persons that you find are the most difficult to disagree with.

6. Learn how to say "I was wrong."
   If, in the middle of a disagreement, you put somebody down or if you later realize that your adamantly held position was

incorrect, acknowledge your mistake. You might say, "I'm sorry for my error" or "I think your evidence is more convincing than mine." The Book of Proverbs speaks to this principle from several angles. "The intelligent man is always open to new ideas. In fact, he looks for them." (Proverbs 18:15 TLB) "A rebel doesn't care about the facts. All he wants to do is yell." (Proverbs 18:2 TLB) "The selfish man quarrels against every sound principle of conduct by demanding his own way." (Proverbs 18:1 TLB)

7. *Agree to disagree.*

   There are times when people close to you will simply not agree with your opinion. At that point, you can "agree to disagree" instead of getting locked into a win-lose type of battle. We just can't agree with each other on *every* subject. Accept that fact and you'll save yourself much misery in life.

Small Beginnings

1. Play "devil's advocate" in a small group.
2. When someone states an opinion you disagree with slightly, say so.
3. When someone interprets something you said and they are wrong, tell them so.
4. If a friend expresses a different opinion on a movie or book, state your opinion.

Now add some of your own. Make them even more workable than the ones I've listed by utilizing the concepts *what*, *how*, and *when* from the first chapter.

5. _____

6. _____

Be Able to Say No

Working at a University I have been under
constant pressure to serve on numerous
committees, task forces, and pilot groups. No
matter what these little groups are called they
mean two things: extra work and extra time. I
can handle a few committees but when I become
too involved in too many committees, I lose sight
of my mission as a University professor; that of
teaching and scholarly activity. About a year
ago I decided I was serving on enough of these
"problem-solving" groups and that I would form
a policy of saying "no" to any further requests
for committee work.

I immediately called several offices that might
make such requests and stated the following: "I
would like your office to know in advance that I
will not be able to take on any more committee
assignments for this academic year. So if you
are thinking about me for such an assignment,
you should consider an alternative. I am already
serving on several committees and feel I can
only do justice to their activities if I remain at
my present work load." So I warned these
offices in advance that I would be saying "no" to
their requests.

And lucky me! About three days later I
received a call from one of the very offices I had
warned in advance. The receptionist began with
flattery: "We have a committee assignment for
you that fits your skills like a glove. We could

think of no other person to call who would have the expertise which you have to bring to this policy-making group. And the Dean (she's putting some weight behind this) would be very pleased if you would take it." My reply went something like, "I'm very flattered (took a few knots of wind out of her sails) that you and the Dean think so highly of my skills, but as I stated to you three days ago over the telephone I simply cannot take any more assignments." The conversation continued:

Receptionist: "This appointment might really help you in terms of promotion, etc."

Me: "The Dean has already stated to me that he is most pleased with my work as a teacher and scholar. In order to continue as a productive faculty member I simply cannot spread myself too thin. If I do I'll not do any of my job tasks very well."

Receptionist: (She's not ready to give up just yet) "We just can't think of anyone else who will fill the bill. We would really benefit from your abilities."

Me: "Again I truly appreciate your dilemma and your confidence in me and in order to continue as a productive faculty member I simply must limit my committee assignments at this time. Tell the Dean that I really appreciate his thinking of me and that I know how difficult it is to find committee members, but that I cannot take the position."

Receptionist: (One last effort) "Okay, I'll tell the Dean!"

Me: "Thank you" (in a friendly tone).

In this interchange I followed several guidelines which are important in saying "no:"

1. *Warn people in advance that you are going to say no.* This prepares people for your eventual action. It also gives you the opportunity to begin to say your "no" in a less anxiety producing situation. It tends to discourage people from asking you for the favor or request. Advance warning may also cut down the hope which the other person has of getting what they want. Thus that person may be less persistent.

2. *Use the "broken record."* Each time the receptionist utilized a different strategy to convince me, I esssentially repeated in similar words what my position was. This kept me on target. I did not get sidetracked. When she said "we just can't think of anyone else," by suggesting someone else whom she could disagree with. I merely reiterated that I could not accept the position and why. After three "broken records" she took my "no" for an answer. Some people have to hear your "no" only once, others will need to hear it five or six times before they take you seriously. The point is to keep repeating it and don't get sidetracked into other issues.

3. *Validate the requestors dilemma.* By saying, "I truly appreciate your dilemma" and "I know how difficult it is to find committee members," I was validating feelings that the receptionist had about her task. I was caring enough to at least communicate to her that I was listening to her and could appreciate her plight. I genuinely empathized with her, yet that did not mean I

was obligated to say "yes."

Why do I believe that saying "no" is such an important thing to be able to do? Because some of the world's greatest martyrs are persons who aren't able to say "no." These individuals often complain that others take advantage of them or that they never have time for themselves or their families. Yet they miss the fact that they are responsible for their own lives and that it is their perfect right to say "no."

Another reason why this assertive skill is so important is that continued favors tend to become rights. If I hadn't at some point stood my ground on the committee work, various offices around the University would have just assumed that it was their right to expect me to say "yes" to all requests. "Schmidt will do it; he never says no to anything," would have been heard often when administrators were putting together some new task force. And once it's assumed that you will behave in a particular way, it's twice as difficult to try and change.

Saying "no" at the time may be tough. It's too easy to say to yourself, "Oh, it's just not worth the hassle; I'll do it. That way no one will be upset with me. Besides a good person must do favors for others." Let's take a look at these words for a moment. First, you say it's just not worth the hassle. But what kind of hassles do you run into when you've said "yes" to something that you absolutely dread doing? Don't you have just as many, if not more hassles then? And usually the thing you've said "yes" to lasts longer than a simple "no" would have taken.

How many times have you said "yes" to a request you wanted to say "no" to, and later, had to turn it down anyway. And usually you have to back out just before you were to perform the favor. How pleased do you think that other person was at that point? Or perhaps you went along with the request and either were extremely unenthusiastic or did a poor job. How do you think the other individual feels about that kind of response?

Finally, what about the phrase "A good person must do favors for others." True, if I am to have some close relationships I will want to do favors for others. However, if I don't set priorities for my time and energy by saying "yes" to some things and "no" to others then I will have relinquished control of my life. By saying "yes" to all demands from the outside, without making my own decisions about those demands, I have no plan for my own living. Can I be a good person if I say "yes" to so many outside demands that I end up neglecting my job, my family, my marriage, or my relationship with God? How can I expect my children to become responsible adults, who are able to make value judgments and say "no" to immoral acts, when they see me completely controlled by the external world?

Offer Alternatives

In my bout with the Dean's office I did not offer any alternative names that the receptionist might call and ask to be on the committee. I value my friendships with my colleagues too much for that! However, this can be a further step to take when saying "no" to someone. For example, your spouse has just asked you to talk with her. But you are looking forward to a short, refreshing, nap at that particular time. You had a very demanding day at the office and really need a breather. You might say something like, "I can tell from the sound of your voice that whatever you want to talk about is really important. I've had a really demanding day and I'd like just ten minutes to relax and get my thoughts together. I'll be in a lot better shape to talk in just a few minutes." In this way you didn't put your spouse off indefinitely. Instead, you have offered an alternative time to talk ten minutes from now. Both of your rights as individuals have been honored in this way.

Let's look at some other examples, along with possible responses that offer alternatives:

Sally (to a girl friend): "Would you like to go see a movie tonight?"

Mary: "No, Sally I don't care to go out tonight. How about going to a movie on Friday night?"

In this way Mary is saying to Sally, "Look, I value our friendship enough to want to go out with you somewhere soon, but tonight I just don't care to go anywhere."

Here's another example:

Son to Father: "Dad, can we go fishing today?"

Father: "I can't today, son. I just don't have the time. But tell you what, I'll take off early Friday and we'll go up to the Blue River for the afternoon. How does that sound to you?"

Probably pretty good! And certainly much better than "sorry I just don't have the time." Of course this father had better be able to go on Friday. And his statement had better not be designed just to appease his son temporarily.

A Final Word or Two About "No"

First, if you are able to say "no" when you mean no, it follows that others will know you really mean it when you say, "yes." Second, it is your right not to have to explain why you're saying "no." You can just say, "No, I don't care to," if you wish. The need for an explanation depends on the situation, people involved and whether or not you wish to offer alternatives or to validate the other person's feelings.

Remember:

1. Warn people that you will say "no."
2. Use the broken record response.
3. Validate the other person.
4. Offer Alternatives, if you wish.

Keep In Touch With Friends

Working as a professor can become very demanding. There are many other activities besides teaching which occupy a professor's time. Very quickly it becomes rather easy to isolate myself in my work and not have enough time for coffee breaks, chitchats with colleagues or lunch. A couple of years ago I found myself in this position. I was busily struggling for a promotion through publications, doing a good job of teaching, serving on several dissertation committees and heading task forces, along with a few other things. Then one morning I came across this quote in the newspaper:

> "To let friendship die away by negligence and silence is certainly not wise. It is voluntary to throw away one of the greatest comforts of this weary pilgrimage."
> —Johnson

These words hit home like a jackhammer! I decided to do two things:

1. I would have lunch with my colleagues at least twice per week. That meant if I were to ask one person for lunch and they turned me down I would ask another person and another until I had two luncheon engagements arranged for that week.

2. I would organize an informal "feelings" meeting among interested faculty on a weekly basis. This meant getting together for about an hour over coffee to discuss our concerns and celebrations for that week.

The next day I set up my two luncheons for the week. And after night class that evening I entered a professor's office where several of my colleagues were gathered. Each person in the room looked tired and upset. I reflected, "you people look as worn out as I feel." There were several affirmative sighs. I suggested the weekly "feelings" gathering and everyone enthusiastically agreed to trying it. This began a series of relief-giving, sharing times together.

I remembered what one of my students had said, "Friendships are not bookkeeping arrangements. If you want to spend some time with a friend, just do it. Don't worry about whether that person contacted you last or whether it's 'your turn' or not." She was right. When I began to express my feelings of isolation with other faculty members they owned up to feeling exactly the same way. Several of them admitted that they were sitting around waiting for others to make the initial contact or that they felt it was someone else's turn to initiate contact. Meanwhile, most of us were miserable and secluded from each other, keeping our books; "let's see, I called him last. Now it's his turn to ask me for coffee."

Keeping in touch with friends helps you receive the "strokes," "warm fuzzies," and the fun times that you need in order to function. Being with a friend also helps when you're down. A friend a day keeps depression away. And people are usually pleased when you contact them. Paul sums it up very nicely in II Timothy 1:7: "For the Holy Spirit, God's gift, does not want you to be afraid of people, but to be wise and strong, and to love them and enjoy being with them" (TLB).

So if you're sitting there wanting to be with someone you like, give that friend a call, now. If that person is not home, don't give up. Call again in an hour. Or if that person has plans and can't be with you when you'd like, set up an alternative time when you can get together.

Avoid saying things to yourself like, "They refused my dinner invitation because I'm a terrible host," or "He didn't call me, therefore he doesn't care for me." More often than not these thoughts are simply erroneous. Look at the facts. Are you a terrible host? Who has told you this? How many people have told you just the opposite? Perhaps he didn't call you because he's been out of town, or busy with work. Give him a break. Call him. Give yourself and him some comfort, some fun, and some enjoyment. Keep in touch with friends. They're God's gift.

6

Your Thought Life

Men are not worried by
things,
but by their ideas about things.
When we meet with difficulties, become
anxious and troubled,
let us not blame
others, but rather
ourselves, that is:
our idea about things.
— *Epictetus*

A major research project at Stanford University pointed to two critical variables in helping people change during the process of group psychotherapy. First, the group leader must be empathetic. The leader must be able to tune in to what others are saying. Second, and even more important, the group must serve the function of helping participants gain more constructive and meaningful philosophies of life. That is, the group that is successful will give people a better way of thinking about life.

There is physiological evidence that sensations and perceptions that we receive or take in from the world around us are first absorbed and interpreted in the thinking centers of the brain before these same sensations are allowed to be transferred to the emotional centers. Thus, we interpret and think about sensations before we develop a feeling about them. It follows, then, that our thoughts dramatically affect our feelings and actions.

What do you think about? That suggests Proverbs 23:7 as a man "thinks within himself, so he is" (NASB). H. Norman Wright in a helpful book called *Improving Your Self-Image*[1] states:

> "As we build up storehouses of memories, knowledge, and experiences we seem to retain and remember those things which we concentrate upon the most. If we concentrate upon rejection and hurt, they will be a part of our experience. Each person is responsible for the things he allows his mind to dwell upon."

We are told in Philippians 4:8 what we are to think about: "Finally, brethren, whatever is true, whatever is honorable, whatever is just, whatever is pure, whatever is lovely, whatever is gracious, if there is any excellence, if there is anything worthy of praise, think about these things" (RSV). Colossians 3:2 advises that we should set our minds and keep them set on what is above—the higher things—not on the things that are on the earth.

Herman Gockel writes in *Answer To Anxiety* about your thought life:

> "There is much more to this whole business than merely getting rid of negative or unworthy thoughts. In fact, the concept of 'getting rid' is itself a sign of

negative thinking. We shall succeed in this whole matter, not in the measure in which we *fill* them with thoughts that are wholesome and uplifting. The human mind can never be a vacuum. He who thinks he can improve the tenants of his soul simply by evicting those that are unworthy will find that for every unworthy tenant he evicts through the back door, several more will enter through the front. It is also a matter of screening, selecting, admitting, and cultivating those tenants that have proved themselves desirable."[2]

There you have it again. The principle of *increasing positive things as opposed* to decreasing negative things is basic to life.

Thought Patterns Can Be Changed

The scripture promises that negative thinking can be changed to positive thinking. In Ephesians 4:23 we are told, "Now your attitudes and thoughts must all be constantly changing for the better." (TLB) This is to be a continuing experience. Paul said in Romans 12:2, "And do not be conformed to this world, but be transformed by the renewing of your mind . . . " (NASB) The Word renewal here means "to make new from above." This implies that your thought life can be renovated through prayer, searching God's Word and believing in the working of the Holy Spirit.

In the background of Paul's writings is his conception of the Christian's growing likeness to

Christ. Thus, in order to find out the direction your thought life ought to be moving, do an intensive study of Christ's life. Read the four Gospels, Matthew, Mark, Luke, and John. Use a good Bible reference such as *The Interpreter's One-Volume Commentary on the Bible.* Based upon your study, make a list of the kinds of thoughts that Christ probably had as he moved through his own life. These are the kinds of thoughts that we ought to be clinging to and constantly thinking.

We are, in fact, commanded by Paul to let our minds be filled with the mind of Christ. In Philippians 2:5 he directs us, "Let this mind be in you, which was also in Christ Jesus." (KJV) The major point here is clear. We are to reflect in our own minds the mind of Jesus Christ. Whatever he thought about we are to be thinking about as well.

My Mother-in-Law, Myrtle Lambert, died of cancer a little over two years ago. During her struggle with this dread disease, she constantly turned to a particular Scripture passage which tells us what to *stop* thinking about and what to *begin* thinking about. "Do not fret or have any anxiety about anything, but in every circumstance and in everything by prayer and petition with thanksgiving continue to make your wants known to God. And God's peace which transcends all understanding, shall garrison and mount guard over your hearts and minds in Christ Jesus. For the rest, brethren, whatever is true, whatever is worthy of reverence and is honorable and seemly, whatever is just, whatever is pure, whatever is lovely and lovable, whatever is kind and winsome and gracious, if there is any virtue and excellence, if there is anything worthy of praise, think on and weigh and take account of these things—fix your minds on them. Practice what you have learned and received and heard and seen in me. And model your way of living on it, and the God of peace—of untroubled, undisturbed well-being will be with you" (Philippians 4:6-9, Amplified).

Self-Talk

Imagine that you're out on a date with that special person and you're in a restaurant. Your date has been paying you undivided attention up to this point. All of a sudden he turns to the people at the next table and begins a conversation with them. What thoughts go through your mind? What does your self-talk sound like? Perhaps you say to yourself, "He must find me so boring that he can't continue talking with me . . . He's ignoring me, deliberately!" And what feelings would build up inside of you as you think these things? You would perhaps feel rejected, inferior, and angry. What sort of actions would follow? You might sulk, glare at him or become silent.

What if, instead of having these thoughts, you talked to yourself in the following manner? "It's neat that he's so friendly with others" . . . "I think I'll join in the conversation." Chances are with that sort of thinking you'd feel warm inside and warm toward your date. You would probably begin talking with the others at the next table. It's unlikely that you would sulk or become silent and morose.

Perhaps you've expressed anger toward someone recently, and as you did, you were also thinking, "she probably thinks I'm a witch . . . she'll never speak to me again . . . I'm sure she will not be my friend ever again . . . It's a sin to express my anger." With this kind of thinking what would you be feeling? Most likely you'd begin to feel embarrassed, ashamed, perhaps a bit depressed and discouraged. As a result, you might refrain from contacting your friend. It's conceivable that you'd act sullen and non-communicative around that person. If that were to occur the other person might very well receive the message that you're still angry and upset and that you do not wish to continue the friendship.

In contrast let's say that you begin thinking, "I don't like being angry . . . but I'm not stuck with it . . . my thoughts and feelings are important . . . it's okay to express them . . . the Bible says 'If you are angry, don't sin by nursing your grudge. Don't let the sun go down with you still angry . . . get over it quickly' (Ephesians 4:26 TLB) . . . being angry at someone doesn't have to lead to a loss of friendship . . . I've been angry toward that person before and we remained friends, why not now also . . . Christ became angry from time to time, even with his disciples, but they still loved each other . . . I'll call her now and clear the air." Saying these things to yourself would probably have a contrasting effect upon your feelings and your behavior. It is likely that you'd be talking to your friend again, soon, and that forgiveness and reconciliation would occur.

When asked why she was depressed, a young woman stated that her husband had left her. She thought that the rejection was causing her depression. When we looked further this was not the real case of her depression. Instead, it was her subjective interpretation, or *self-talk*, that was responsible for her *extreme* feelings of dejection and hopelessness. "This is awful," she thought. "I'll never be able to make it on my own. I must be really undesirable for him to leave me. No one could ever love me again. It's *all* my fault. I drove him away. I'd probably drive anyone away. I'm a complete failure. There's something drastically wrong with me." True, she had experienced something most unpleasant. Separation and divorce is very much like experiencing the death of a loved one. However, before this woman could begin to enjoy living again, she had to change her thinking patterns regarding the loss of her husband. And when she did her thoughts sounded more like the following: "I am sad because of this situation. I wish strongly that it could have worked out. I will miss him terribly. This is most unfortunate, but it is not the end of my life. We tried everything humanly possible to hold our relationship together. Even eight months of marriage counseling proved futile. I'll pick up the pieces and go on from here."

Each of these examples point out that our feelings and actions are not influenced as much by events as they are by our interpretations of these events. It then follows that what we need to do is to change our interpretations of events from unrealistic, irrational thoughts to more realistic objective truths about these events.

Talking Sense To Yourself

John Lembo, author of *Help Yourself* suggests four steps in the process of "talking sense to yourself." They are:

1. Identify the situation that you find unpleasant.
2. List the ideas that you are telling yourself about the situation.
   a) The awful things that it signifies
   b) the things that should happen
3. Challenge the self-talk in terms of the facts about yourself and your world.
4. Work to improve what can be improved and accepting what cannot.[3]

1. *Stating the unpleasant situation*

In this part you merely state what circumstance is upsetting you. Is it your own or someone else's failure or mistake? Perhaps you're upset over an unfortunate set of circumstances. Here are some examples:

"I'm upset because I couldn't get the car started this morning."
"I'm extremely disappointed because my classmates criticized my report."
"I'm very embarrassed because Mary turned me down for a date."
"I'm extremely depressed and angry because my boss didn't give me a promotion."

2. Listing self-talk

Now analyze what you are thinking in regard to your unpleasant situation. In the example about not being able to start the car, you might be saying, "I know nothing about cars, therefore I'm just plain stupid and I'll always be stupid. It just isn't fair. This car should just start, especially today when everything else is going wrong." If you were saying this you might feel inferior and angry. The resulting behavior might look something like you beating on the steering wheel, avoiding people all day and snapping at your fellow workers.

If your classmates had criticized your report, your negative self-talk might be, "My report wasn't any good. I'm a lousy writer. I shouldn't even be in college. I think I'll quit." With those thoughts you would feel inferiority and disappointment. You might tear up your report and quit school.

If your situation was "being turned down for a date," your thoughts could go something like this: "Women must think I'm undesirable. Obviously I'm unattractive. I'm a real failure with women. I just have nothing to offer." Again, the resulting feelings would probably be depression, embarrassment and inferiority. And you might not phone Mary, or any other girl, for another month or two.

a) The awful things that the situation signifies

In the examples above, some of the "awful

things" that such persons would be telling themselves would include:

"I'm just plain stupid."

"I'm a lousy writer."

"My report is no good."

"I'm unattractive."

"I'm a failure."

"I have nothing to offer."

These are thoughts that relate to *personal mistakes and failures*..

A second category under "awful things" is: What am I telling myself about my unpleasant experiences *with others*. Some examples of this category are:

"My boss is a horrible person. I am always being criticized and insulted by him. He makes me angry every day."

"I must be a worthless person and lousy parent if my children don't obey me."

A third category under "awful things" is: What am I telling myself about *my unfortunate life situation*? Some examples of this category are:

"My job is meaningless, I can't stand it."

"My life is so horrible being blind. I'll never be able to have any enjoyment in life.

b) *The things that should happen*

  1) What am I telling myself about the way *I should perform*?

    a) "Good employees are always on time for work. Therefore, I must always be on time."

    b) "I have to make other people like me at all times."

2.) What am I telling myself about the way *people should treat me?*
    a) "My boyfriend should pay attention to me and to only me."
    b) "Other people should always trust me. They should never question what I'm saying."
3.) What am I telling myself about the way *life should treat me?*
    a) "The world should treat me fairly. I should be as financially well off as anyone else."
    b) "I should have a job that offers the right hours, satisfaction and money."

3.   *Challenging self-talk*

Once you identify the type of negative self-talk you are engaging in, the next step is to challenge these self-defeating thoughts. The way to do this is to "put your thoughts on trial." Asking for evidence that the situation signifies "awful things" or that certain things "should happen." There is no point in gathering evidence, however, unless the type of evidence is relevant to the problem. For example, if you wanted to know if the population of Vermont was over 365,000 what would be the best kind of evidence? It would probably be ridiculous to go around asking what most people thought was the population of Vermont and then accept the average on the stated answers. You would probably want to look in an Almanac, or some other source of authority.

Rian McMullin and Bill Casey, have identified five methods to prove or disprove something. They are:

1. Use your senses (seeing, hearing, tasting, touching, smelling).
2. Ask an authority.
3. Find out what most people think.
4. Use your reasoning and logic.
5. Use your own experience.[4]

The really important point is that while one method is good for some problems, that same method might be ridiculous for another. Let's return to a previous example to illustrate how some of these five methods could be used to challenge your negative self-talk.

Negative Thought:
"I'm just plain stupid." (Person who couldn't get car started) In order to put this thought on trial you might *use your own reasoning and logic* by asking some of the following questions:

What rational basis do I have for telling myself that I'm stupid? I can usually figure things out. How can *one event* in which I don't know something or can't figure something out make me draw the conclusion that I'm stupid? You might also *find out what most people think* by asking these questions:

Where is the evidence that people think I am a complete idiot? Can I read other people's minds to know what they are thinking? Who has ever told me that I'm just plain stupid? What, in fact, do people say regarding my intelligence? Why wouldn't people think I'm simply another fallible human being like everyone else?

Or you could *use your own experience* by asking and answering:

What does my experience tell me about whether I'm an idiot or not? I succeeded in learning how to enclose my patio last year. I graduated from high school, and I succeeded in passing several college courses. That proves that I'm not stupid about some things and that I can learn about things that I don't know about.

Finally, you could *ask an authority:*

What have my teachers told me about my abilities? My professors? What kind of report did my boss turn in on me? She said I was one of her better employees in terms of getting the job done and doing it right. Who says that I should be able to do everything right the first time I try?

Let's look at another example and utilize again some of these methods for examining evidence.

Negative Thought:

"My boss is a horrible person. I am always being criticized and insulted by him. He makes me angry every day." (Employee who is criticized by boss.)

Use your reasoning and logic:

What rational basis do I have for telling myself that my boss is a horrible person? Isn't he just a fallible human being who does things I don't like? Doesn't practically everyone do things that someone doesn't like?

Use your own experience:

Am I always being criticized and insulted? To say that I am always being insulted means that every second I am being met with critical remarks. That's silly. My experience tells me that only occasionally are critical remarks directed toward me.

Countering

Putting your thoughts on trial and examining the evidence leads to a process called countering. When you "counter" an irrational, self-defeating thought you fight it with your reason. By asking some of the questions in the previous section you will discover counters that you can use on a daily basis to counteract irrational thoughts. Here are some examples of irrational thoughts and counters:

Irrational thought: "Since my boss criticized me that means I'm no good."

Counter: "My boss criticizes everybody!" (finding out what most people think)

Counter: "That's the first time he's criticized me in over a week." (Using my experience)

Irrational thought: "She looks like a very interesting person, but she probably wouldn't be interested in me."

Counter: "How do I know? I haven't asked her!" (using my experience)

Counter: "What can I lose by trying to meet her?" (using logic)

Irrational thought: "I'd better not disagree with what they are saying, because then they might not like me."

Counter: "If they don't know what I think

they'll never have a chance to decide whether or not they like me."

Counter: "That puts me in a horrible position, where I can only agree!"

Irrational thought: "Healthy people don't get anxious or upset."

Counter: "In my view, John F. Kennedy was a very healthy person, and he certainly got upset and anxious at times."

Counter: "The Gospels certainly describe Jesus as feeling anxious and upset from time to time. If he wasn't healthy, who was?"

Counters should be statements of reality. In other words, if your irrational thought is, "I am inferior in every way," a poor counter would be "No I'm not, I'm superior in every way." A good counter will usually come from one of the five methods described earlier for putting your thoughts on trial. A realistic counter might come from simply asking other people for feedback about your ability. From this process you might come up with a counter such as, "everyone I asked stated that I was good at several things."

Counters should be personally believable. Your counter could include everything from a scripture passage to a simple "baloney!" The important point here is that you really "buy into" the counters you use. For example, don't just pick a Bible verse because someone else in authority says it's the right one. Find one that speaks directly to you, both personally and emotionally.

Countering can either be done during a difficult situation or as part of what we'll call a rehearsal exercise. Let's talk about the use of counters in real-life situations first. You are about to call an old friend. You give yourself some irrational thoughts like, "I'd like to call my friend, but if she hasn't called me by now, she probably doesn't want to talk to me." Then you remind yourself to counter and begin to actively think to yourself, "That's ridiculous! If I want to talk to her, it's my responsibility to call her!" The result is that you call your friend, she is delighted that you did and you end up setting a luncheon date.

The counters that you use on the spot should be as active and persuasive as possible. Shout them out in your head! Scream internally at those self-defeating thoughts! Use several arguments for each irrational thought.

All the counters used in this chapter are *agruments with thoughts, not emotions.* That's why a counter such as, "No, I'm not sad" is a poor one. That kind of agrument only hides feelings and is potentially harmful. A better counter for "sadness" would be to attack the self-defeating *thoughts* which are leading you to escalate your sadness and make the situation worse than is warranted. Perhaps something like this would be better: "I'm sad because I failed to get the job I applied for, but that does not mean that I will never find work. I have other alternatives to interview for tomorrow." Argue with the thought, not the feeling.

Let's take another on-the-spot countering example. You haven't had any vacation time for quite a spell. You feel the doldrums setting in and you want to ask for some time off. Yet some irrational thoughts are holding you back: "If I ask for vacation time, my boss will probably think I'm a lazy good-for-nothing and I'll blow any chance for a raise." At that point you begin to counter aggressively and realistically: "I've never seen him respond that way to anyone. Besides, I'm just mind reading. I do not have information that supports these self-defeating thoughts. Furthermore, vacation time is my right. I've earned it. I need it for myself and for my family!"

If you have difficulty coming up with good, sound arguments against irrational thoughts, here are two things you might try. One, think of someone you know who handles troublesome situations well. What do they probably say to themselves that triggers them to act appropriately in that kind of situation? How would that person argue with you if you told him or her your irrational thought? Two, go ahead and actually ask that person for some counters or arguments.

Countering Practice

I Peter 1:13 tell us, "gird your minds for action . . . " (NASB). The words refer to "mental exertion." This implies a very active, aggressive approach to filling our minds with positive, fulfilling thoughts. It's hard work to re-train our heads to say more constructive things than we've been used to. And it takes practice! Here are more situations with their accompanying negative self-thoughts and resulting self-defeating feelings and behaviors. A few counters for each negative thought are included. Add some counters of your own for practice.

Situation:
Belinda is unhappy because someone she is very close to is moving to another city.
Negative thought:
"I should be happy all the time. Christians are not to be unhappy."
Resulting feelings:
Unworthiness, ashamed.
Resulting behavior:
Belinda does not express to her friend that she will miss her. Her friend gets the picture that Belinda doesn't care that she's leaving.

Counters: (arguments against the negative thought)
1. "That's nonsense! I can't think of one Biblical character who was happy all the time."
2. "That thought is a great way to lose friends fast!"
3. "That's dumb! I'm trying to be God."
4. "Whoever told me that? My pastor certainly has never suggested it!"
5. (You add one)_____
6. (Another)_____

Situation:
Mike is sitting alone in his apartment. Several things have gone wrong for him this week and he'd like to be able to get some support from someone, but he hesitates.
Negative Thought:
"Strong people don't ever ask for help."

Resulting feelings:
Extreme loneliness, dejection
Resulting behavior:
Mike stays in his apartment all weekend. He gets drunk Saturday night and stays drunk for most of Sunday.

Counters:

1. "Moses asked for help from God continually. He asked for help from Aaron to be able to speak to the Israelites. And Moses was chosen by God because of his strength."
2. "Other people I know ask for help continually."
3. "I often help other people with their problems. Aren't I entitled to the same?"
4. "It's okay not to be perfect."
5. "This thought only hurts me."
6. (Your turn!)_____
7. (Again)_____

Situation:
Sally Harried feels that she needs some time just for herself away from her children, yet she does nothing to make this happen.
Negative Thought:
"My children and my husband will think I'm terribly selfish if I ask to have some time to be left alone."
Resulting feelings:
Resentment, depressed resignation.
Resulting behavior:
Sally remains at home, becomes more upset with her children, begins shouting at them

more frequently. One day she beats one of the children, leaving bruises.

Counters:
1. "I have a right to some time alone."
2. Having some time away from the children will help me come back to them refreshed at the end of the day."
3. "I have no reason to believe that they will think I'm selfish."
4. "The Gospels report many instances when Jesus needed to be alone. He's my example!"

5. _____

6. _____

Situation:
Ellen's daughter wants to borrow the car whenever she pleases.

Negative thought:
"My daughter will probably hate me if I don't let her use the car whenever she wants."

Resulting feeling:
Scared

Resulting behavior:
Ellen allows her daughter to take the car when she pleases.

Counters:
1. "I have a right to say 'no.' It's my car!"
2. "She will not respect me as a parent unless I stand up for what I believe in!"
3. "This thought will lead me to act in ways that I don't want!"
4. "In the long run, that kind of thinking will only hurt my relationship with her!"

5. "Disagreeing with someone does not always lead to quarrelling and fights."

6. _____

7. _____

Rehearsal exercises

Let's take one step backward before you jump into a troublesome situation in which you normally do some irrational thinking. There are several ways you can "rehearse" a more positive way of approaching these difficult predicaments.

1. Think ahead of time about an approaching episode that will be tough for you to handle. Write down what some of your self-defeating thoughts are in that situation. Now, write down as many counters as you can think of which argue against these irrational thoughts. Memorize the most powerful counters you come up with. Write them **on a note** card and carry the card with you when you go into that situation. Read through the list of counters just before you begin action.

2. Get yourself into a relaxed position (in an easy chair, etc.). Allow yourself to let go of tension for a few moments. Now imagine yourself in the approaching troublesome scene. Make the scene as "real" as possible. "See" the colors and shapes; "hear" the sounds; notice details in your imagined scene. Now go ahead and say the negative thought that you get in that situation. Next say the word "stop," "get away from me," "quit bugging me," or "what a stupid thought." (What you are doing here

is punishing the self-defeating thought). Now begin to counter as aggressively as you can. Really go after your irrational thinking. Mentally shout your best counters. Some people even say them out loud. Do this for about 30 seconds. Do this entire sequence about 15 times before a given problem encounter.

3. Add one further step to exercise 2. After you have countered for about 30 seconds, immediately start imagining the best possible consequences of your positive thoughts and your counters. Use your imagination and feel free to exaggerate. For example, "If I can realize that making mistakes is not awful, that it only shows I'm human I'll begin to take a few more risks. I'll begin to trust God more. If I learn to trust Him more I'll probably be a lot more at ease about life. I won't be so uptight and careful about everything I say and do. I'll experience more freedom. I'll be much more fun to be around, others will respond to me more favorably . . . " Keep on doing this. When you have imagined about all of the positive outcomes that could develop from your positive thoughts you can stop.

4. Reward yourself internally each time you use a counter in a real situation. Say something to yourself like, "that was neat," "I did it," "praise the Lord," or "that's more like it." If you practice this kind of "rehearsal" you will be surprised at how powerful they are. If you stop and think about it, how many times do you rehearse in your mind how horrible some coming event is going to be? If we have

taught ourselves to behave in negative ways by rehearsing negatively, how about positive rehearsals?

5. *Improving what can be improved*

> May I be granted the strength to accept
> the things I cannot change
> The courage to change the things I can
> And the wisdom to know the difference.
> —A.A. Prayer

Once you have challenged the "awful things" a particular situation signifies and the things that "should happen," you can begin to implement a better course of action. You do this by silently giving yourself directions. These self-directions guide you to act and feel more constructively.

Here are some examples:

Situation: At a church picnic you see someone you don't know, but would like to meet.
Self-direction: "I'd like to introduce myself. I'll walk up to him and say 'hello, my name is . . .' "
Reaction: Feeling more confident, assertive. You introduce yourself.

Situation: Bobby, your five year old, has just taken the magic marker to the kitchen floor. You're tempted to scream, yell and hit him. However, you know that kind of response hasn't helped in the past.
Self-direction: "My purpose with my children is to teach, not punish."
Reaction: You get out the Mr. Clean and a rag and have Bobby clean up his own mess without yelling, screaming or hitting. Bobby experiences

the consequences of his own actions and never again writes on the floor.

Situation: You are going for a job interview. You know that it is important for you to make a good impression.
Self-direction: "Stand up straight. Look them in the eye."
Reaction: Your posture is good throughout the interview. You look at the interviewers while they are talking and while you are speaking.

Situation: You have successfully handled a difficult situation with your daughter.
Self-direction: "Reward yourself."
Reaction: You say something to yourself like, "that's the idea, I'm getting better." You feel good inside. You add another pound to your self-image.

Situation: You and your boyfriend are having a discussion about an important topic that affects your relationship.
Self-direction: "Be open."
Reaction: You are straight with him and the lines of communication are strengthened. You feel relieved and strong.

Here are some more *self-directions* which may apply to some of your own life situations:

"Catch them being good." (children, employees)
"Calm down."
"Relax a bit."
"Stick to the issue."
"Try it, you might like it."
"Look for the facts."

"I'll wait until I've calmed down."
"Be gentle."
"Express your feelings."
"Be friendly."
"Be patient. Listen to what they have to say."
"Speak up."
"Listen."
"Pay attention."
"Show affection."
"Be firm."
"Think rationally."
"Look on the bright side."
"Hang in there."
"Try it once more."
"Praise the Lord."
"Forgive him."
"Tell her you love her."
"Quit feeling sorry for yourself."
"Pray."
"Look up."
"Give yourself some credit."

NOW ADD A FEW OF YOUR OWN:

_____

_____

_____

These self-directions should be clear and to the point. You might even use a rehearsal exercise for these, by:

1. Sit down and relax.
2. Clearly imagine an applicable scene.
3. Imagine that you are saying the appropriate self-direction to yourself.

4. Visualize yourself calmly and confidently following your self-direction.
5. Repeat this entire process five times at each sitting.
6. Follow steps 1 through 5 at least four times per day.

After you've practiced through rehearsal, start using the self-directions in real life. Praise the Lord and yourself when you succeed in following your own directions!

The Things You Cannot Change

At times we all experience things that we cannot change. I have known two blind psychologists over the past seven years. Neither one of them could do anything to change the fact that they cannot "see." Yet both of them are developing their talents to the best of their abilities. They are both absorbed in doing the things that they can do and that gives them great satisfaction. They are not focusing on the disadvantages of being blind. It is our point of focus that counts. As a man "thinks within himself, so he is." (Proverbs 23:7 NASB).

In a recent research study, some scientists selected three groups at random to shoot basketballs from the standard free throw line. All groups were approximately equal in basket-shooting ability. Then one group was allowed to go home. A second group was given hours of practice shooting free throws. The third group was given the same amount of time to *just think about* making free throws successfully. What do you think the results were? The group that was sent home did not improve their basket-making ability. The group that had actual practice improved significantly. And the group who merely *thought about* shooting free throws correctly also improved significantly! In fact they improved roughly as much as those who had direct practice! Do I have to say anymore about the possibilities of correct thinking?

1. Norman Wright. *Improving Your Self-Image*. (Irvine, California: Harvest House, 1977).
2. Herman Gockel, *Answer to Anxiety* (St. Louis: Concordia, 1965), p. 156.
3. John Lembo. *Help Yourself* (Niles, Illinois: Argus Communications 1974).
4. R. McMullin and B. Casey. *Talk Sense To Yourself*. (Lakewood, Colorado: Creative Designs, 1975).

7

Relaxation: Allowing Worry and Anxiety to Fade

Happiness is like a butterfly;
The more you chase it, the more it will
elude you.
But if you turn your attention to other
things,
It comes and softly sits on your shoulder.
                              —L. Richard Lessor

It's rush hour. You're sitting impatiently inside your late model sedan, creeping along at a snail's pace. You're already late for this evening's activities. That last customer at work decided right at 5 o'clock that he'd just take his sweet old time. And now you're churning inside, anxious and upset.

Now you are nervously awaiting the end of the the introduction of the evening's speaker, which happens to be you. Your mind suddenly goes blank. You panic for a moment, the first trickle of sweat running down your side. You try to focus only on the friendly faces in the audience, yet you have a feeling of dread and fear.

Or you're rushing around the house, frantically picking up after your children, thinking, "I've got three couples coming for dinner in two hours, and I'm not half ready for them yet. How will I ever get done in time?"

We truly live in an "Age of Anxiety." And there are no magic solutions which can make any of us immune to the pace and stress of our modern world. Although psychological research indicates that a certain amount of arousal or anxiety is productive, in that it motivates us to act, a high amount of stress usually keeps us from functioning as we would like. It certainly prevents us from performing as well as we are capable.

The Effects Of Anxiety

Wayne Dyer, the well known author and lecturer, has stated:

> You could take the ten best worriers in the entire world. Put them in the same room for the rest of their lives and allow them to worry and worry only. And you know what would happen? Absolutely nothing!

God's Word has some things to say about the effects of worry and anxiety: "I heard and my (whole inner self) trembled, my lips quivered at the sound. Rottenness enters into my bones and under me—down to my feet . . . " (Habakkuk 3:16 Amplified). Proverbs 12:25 says, "Anxiety in a man's heart weighs it down." (Amplified). That certainly describes the feelings that anxious individuals relate to me in my counseling office. They actually feel as if there is a heaviness pushing on their body. They feel helpless and overwhelmed.

There are physiological effects as well. People experience:

headaches
backaches
increased perspiration
weakness and fatigue
shortness of breath
constriction in the chest
indigestion
butterflies in the stomach
diarrhea
"pounding heart"
menstrual irregularity
insomnia
muscular tension

When we are anxious, our attention is impaired and our mental activities are interferred with. We have poor concentration and judgment. There is a good deal of interference with the efficiency and effectiveness of our mental functioning, especially as tasks become more complex. Thus, important problem-solving skills are reduced to a minimum when we are highly anxious.

There is an old Moorish proverb that states: "He who is afraid of a thing gives it power over him." Worry and fear can become self-fulfilling prophecies. Job 3:25-26 says, "For the thing that I fear comes upon me, and what I dread befalls me." (RSV) Statistics show that if you are the type of person who worries about having accidents, you are the most likely candidate for such a mishap. One person says, "What if I forget what my notes mean? What if they ask a question I can't answer? What if they start complaining about my speech? What if some of them fall asleep?" The other person says, "I'm nervous about this speech, but that's normal. I've yet to meet someone who has said that they do not get anxious about giving talks. I'm well prepared. I'll just take my time, tell them what I know, and go from there." Which one do you suppose would be the most successful public speaker?

Small Beginnings in Overcoming Anxiety

Earl Nightengale, a researcher, found that 40 percent of our worries are about things that never happen. Another 30 percent concern things that are in the past, that can't be changed by worry. Still another 12 percent are needless worries about our health. And 10 percent of our worries Nightengale designated as "petty, miscellaneous worries"—not worth worrying about. That leaves a total of 8 percent for real, legitimate concerns! So let's look at some ways to deal with the 92 percent of *illegitimate* worries and anxieties.

Using Scripture

One of the simplest, most effective strategies for dealing with anxiety is through the use of God's Word. On one side of a 3x5 note card write the word STOP, GO AWAY, or QUIT BUGGING ME. On the other side of the card write out Philippians 4:6-9. Use either the Amplified or The Living Bible versions. Keep the card with you at all times. Whenever you begin to worry, pull out the card. Read the word STOP! Say it aggressively as you did with the counters in the last chapter. If you are alone say it out loud, if with people, scream it internally! Then turn the card over and read those beautiful verses in their entirety. Relish each word as you read it. Let the truth of these words really sink in! The effect this will have is to first punish or break the chain of worry by giving yourself the cue to STOP. Then you will *replace* the anxiety and irrational thoughts with some alternative thinking from the Lord.

As I work with persons in counseling I've been most excited by the positive results of this technique. After a week or so you might be able to go through this process without the card. This is a good way to memorize Scripture that can be useful to you in many areas of daily living. You don't have to limit its use to anxiety or worry. Use it to work on other negative emotions like depression or guilt. Just pick some Scripture passages that really speak to you in a helpful way with regard to these emotions. Then write them down on a note card.

With regard to the emotions of anxiety and worry the following passages might also be helpful to you:

I Peter 5:7 (NASB)
Psalms 37: 1, 3-5, 7 Amplified
Proverbs 15:15 Amplified
Psalms 34 (TLB)
Isaiah 41:10 RSV
Isaiah 43:1 RSV
Isaiah 43:2-3 RSV
Romans 5:1 TLB
John 16:33 TLB

Isaiah 26:3 TLB
Matthew 6:34 TLB

Books

There are several books dealing specifically with anxiety which I find helpful. They are:

1. Gockel, Herman. *Answer to Anxiety*, concordia Publishing House, St. Louis, Mo., 1965.
2. Lee, Earl. *Recycled for Living.* Regal Books, Division of G/L Publications, Glendale, Ca., 1973.
3. Schmidt, Jerry A. *Help Yourself: A Guide to Self-Change.* Research Press Co., Champaign, Ill., 1976.
4. Wright, Norman. *An Answer to Worry and Anxiety.* Harvest House Publishers, Irvine, Ca., 1976.
5. Wright, H. Norman. *The Christian Use of Emotional Power.* Fleming H. Revell Co., Old Tappan, N.J., 1974.

Prayer

In a most exciting book entitled *The Edge of Adventure,* I came across what has been for me a God-send in my own prayer life. In the book, the authors outline "Seven minutes of time with God." *In the first 30 seconds* you just try to relax. Take a deep breath, and realize that God, who loves you deeply, is there with you. Ask Him to calm your heart and make you receptive to His will. *During the next 4 minutes,* you read in the Gospel of John not for factual information but with two questions in mind:

1. What kind of personality does God—the one to whom I have given my life—have?

2. Is there anything here that speaks to me for today, now?

During the last 2½ minutes—Prayer. They suggest the following order:

1. *Adoration.* Just tell Christ that you love Him—in your own words . . . "I love you, Christ, I want to respond to You with my whole life." A line from a Psalm may be another way to do this. Any expression of praise that comes from the depths of your soul seems to help.

2. *Confession.* What I do here is to lay out to God very specific things that I am genuinely sorry for. I am very specific about what I'm asking forgiveness for.

3. *Thanksgiving.* Again, be specific. This can be a beautiful time of searching for and discovering all the blessings in my own life.

4. *Supplication.* First I pray for others and their needs. And when I get to my own needs I have often prayed "And as for me, Lord, Thy will be done." This simple statement, along with the adoration part of my prayer time has helped me in letting go of my own anxiety and fears.[1]

I often have my prayer time while I am beginning my day, jogging and exercising. That puts some real energy into it!

Controlling Your Thoughts

In the chapter "Your thought Life," I discussed several strategies for controlling your thoughts. Perhaps the most prominent was the technique of countering. Here are some counters that other individuals have used to attack thoughts that have led them to excessive anxiety and worry:

"This thought only hurts me by making me panic."

"All this excessive worry changes nothing!"

"This thought is pointless!"

"Nobody's perfect!"

"Cool it!"

"What am I doing to myself?"

"Everybody makes mistakes!"

"I can only do so much!"

"Tomorrow's another day."

"I've done all I can."

"Let go."

"Let God take it."

"Now wait a minute."

"Before I get carried away I need to think this through some."

"I'm in charge of my own head."

"I'll decide whether I'll panic or not."

"Fear not, for I am with you, be not dismayed, for I am your God; I will strengthen you, I will help you, I will uphold you with my victorious right hand!" (Isaiah 41:10 RSV)

"I have called you by name, you are mine. When you pass through the waters I will be with you; and through the rivers, they shall not overwhelm you; when you walk through fire you shall not be burned, and the flame shall not consume you. For I am the Lord your God." (Isaiah 43:1-3 RSV)

Write the most helpful counters from this list on a note card and carry the card with you. Again, when you are feeling anxious, take out the note card and read the word STOP! on one side of the card. Then turn it over and read your list of counters. Read them through several times, if you need to. When you feel your anxiety level dropping, read through the list once more, then go ahead and continue whatever you're doing. You could post some of your counters in front of you on your desk at work. Tape other counters with accompanying Bible verses on your refrigerator door, bedroom mirror or on the dash of your car. Place these helpful statements wherever you will be sure to see them frequently.

One person I know has recorded his own voice reading counters and portions of Scripture that he finds helpful in warding off worry. He spends his devotional time driving to work in the morning, listening to these calming statements over his cassette recorder. It has helped him cope with his own fears much more effectively.

Relaxing Yourself

Several psychologists have written about the benefits of relaxation training. Such training has helped individuals with insomnia, hypertension, headaches, excessive perspiration, nervous stomach, social anxiety, and irrational fears. There are several methods which you can use to help yourself relax: muscle relaxation training, visual imagery techniques, meditation, biofeedback, and autogenic training (essentially "talking yourself into relaxation").

Muscle Relaxation Training

The purpose of *muscle relaxation training* is

to experience the difference between *tension* and *relaxation* in your muscles. This is done through a series of exercises designed to help you experience this difference.

Sit or lie in as comfortable a position as you can. Make sure that your legs and arms are uncrossed. Remove or loosen any article of clothing that causes you even a slight amount of discomfort. If you wear contacts, it would be best to remove them. It also would be best to do these exercises alone unless others in the room are serious about learning how to relax and will do the exercises with you. While you are in this comfortable position, do the following:

Clench both fists tightly, as if you were squeezing all the juice out of an imaginary orange in each hand. Notice the muscles in your fingers and lower forearm . . . they are tight . . . tense . . . pulling. Clench your fists like this for about five seconds . . . then relax . . . just let your fists go . . . drop the imaginary orange in each hand. Pay attention to the sensation you now have in the muscles of your fingers, hands, and forearms as they relax. There is a sort of flow of relaxation—perhaps a kind of warmth in these muscles. Enjoy this feeling of relaxation for about twenty to thirty seconds. Now, clench your fists again, tightly. Notice the tension, especially in your fingers, and lower forearm. Now release . . . let go . . . just allow the muscles to loosen. The relaxation is not something you make happen, but something you *allow* to happen. Notice the difference between *tension* and *relaxation* in those muscles.

Repeat this procedure a third time.

Now reach out in front of you with both arms . . . stretch forward with your arms . . . like a lazy tomcat. Move your extended arms over your head . . . reach for the sky . . . hold it. Now stretch your arms out to the sides, then back to the overhead position, again out in front of you, and let your arms drop to your lap. Allow the arms to relax. Again feel the release of tension, this time in the muscles of your upper arms, shoulders, and upper back. Enjoy the lack of tension in these muscles as they become more relaxed . . . still more relaxed . . . still more relaxed . . . more relaxed than ever before.

Repeat this procedure again until your upper arms, shoulders, and extreme upper back are quite relaxed. This usually takes from two to four times as do most muscle relaxation exercises.

Add the other muscle relaxation exercises one at a time. The list below tells you which muscles to tighten and relax for each exercise. Remember that each time you do an exercise you should tense the muscle for about five seconds and then let go completely with that muscle group, experiencing the contrasting relaxation for twenty to thirty seconds. Repeat each exercise three times during each relaxation session. (A session will last about twenty minutes.) In order to obtain maximum results you should spend at least one session per day relaxing. The more practice you get in muscle relaxation the easier it will become to control anxiety in everyday life. Ten suggested muscle groups that need to be relaxed during each session are listed below. Don't do any exercises yet. Just read the list and become familiar with it.

Muscle Relaxation Exercises

Muscle Area	Instructions	Tension Location
Hands	Clench and relax both fists.	The back of your hands and your wrists.
Upper arms	Bend your elbows and fingers of both hands to your shoulders and tense the bicep muscles. Relax.	The bicep muscles
Lower arms	Hold both arms straight out and stretch. Relax.	The upper portion of the forearms.
Forehead	Wrinkle your forehead and raise your eyebrows. Relax.	The entire forehead area.
Forehead	Frown and lower your eyebrows. Relax.	The lower part of the forehead, especially in the region between the eyes.
Eyes	Close your eyes tightly and then relax.	The eyelids.
Jaws	Clench your jaws and relax.	The jaws and cheeks.
Tongue	Bring your tongue upward and press it against the roof of your mouth. Relax.	The area in and around the tongue.
Mouth	Press your lips tightly together. Feel the tension, then relax.	The region around the mouth.
Neck	Press your head backward. Roll to right, shift, roll to left, and straighten. Relax.	The muscles in the back of the neck and at the base of the scalp. Right and left sides of neck.
Neck and Jaws	Bend your head forward and press your chin against your chest. Straighten and relax.	The muscles in the front of the neck and around the jaws.
Shoulders	Bring your shoulders upward toward your ears, shrug, and move around. Relax.	The muscles of the shoulders and the lower part of the neck.

Chest	Take a deep breath and hold it for five seconds. Relax.	The entire chest area.
Abdomen	Tighten your stomach muscles and make your abdomen muscles hard. Relax.	The entire abdominal region.
Back	Arch your back from chair. Relax.	Lower back.
Thighs	Press your heels down as hard as you can, then flex your thighs. Relax.	The muscles in the lower part of the thighs.
Legs	Hold both legs out and point your toes away from your face. Relax.	The muscles of the calf.
Legs	Hold both legs out and point your toes toward your head. Relax.	The muscles below the kneecap.
	Relaxed all over with easy breathing.	
	Arise, refreshed.	

When you are familiar with the muscle groups you will need to relax and the method of tensing and relaxing muscles, you are ready to go ahead and try a relaxation session. There are several ways to do this. Since you should not read this book while you are doing the exercises, you may want to stop now and memorize them. Some people have recorded the instructions on audio tape and then played them back while relaxing. Others have had someone read the instructions to them. Remember the following critical points:

1. Allow at least five seconds for tensing the muscle.
2. Allow twenty to thirty seconds for the relaxation phase.
3. Do the exercises in a place where you won't be interrupted for twenty to thirty minutes.
4. Repeat each exercise three times in a row

before proceeding to the next muscle group.

5. For maximum results practice relaxation at least once each day. [2]

Go ahead now. Relax. Get rid of some tension and allow your body to be recharged. Think of your relaxation period as your time for yourself. Close your eyes and relax. Enjoy the quiet and peacefulness.

What next?

After about a week of relaxing once per day, you can begin to drop some of the tensing exercises and merely tell your muscles to relax. It's not something you force or make happen. Just say to yourself, "I'm going to let my arms relax, go heavy and loose . . . the muscles in my neck are loosening like the strings on a guitar . . I'll allow them to loosen." Once you are able to do this with most of your muscles, you can begin to use these exercises in real-life situations.

You could use relaxation at a social gathering. Let's say that you are a bit tense about meeting new people. You feel a little uptight. You might tighten your hands and arm muscles, briefly . . . and let go. Take a deep breath . . . hold it . . . and let it out. Then you could say to yourself, "I'll let my stomach muscles relax . . . I'll just allow them to loosen." At this point, your anxiety has dropped some. Instead of concentrating on your nervous feeling you turned your attention to relaxation.

Visual Imagery Techniques

Once you have learned to relax your muscles

you can use visual imagery to enhance your relaxation. For example, while you are relaxing, imagine yourself (with your eyes closed) experiencing a very calm, serene scene. See yourself in that scene as being tranquil—at peace. This imagined scene could be you lying in the sand at a beach, with the warm rays of the sun beating down on you. You hear the sounds of sea gulls in the distance and of the waves gently rolling up on the shoreline. Notice the details in your scene. Vividly "see" the colors, shapes of things, sounds, smells—and anything which tends to encourage you to relax still further. The scene should not include any people you know, nor should it involve any active movement or excitement, just peacefulness. Once you have settled on a particular scene as being the most effective, stick with it. It is important to have one scene that you keep using. That scene will become a trigger to produce in you a completely relaxed state. Some other examples of calm scenes you could use include:

1. In the country meadow watching a pond, hearing the crickets and smelling the fresh country air.
2. Walking slowly through the woods on a crisp, fall day.
3. Looking at the lights of a city from a distance.
4. Sitting in front of a fireplace. It's snowing outside and the fire warms you.

Again, after about a week of using this visual imagery technique, try it out in a real situation that arouses only a minimal amount of anxiety. Perhaps, you're thinking about taking a class at a University. You feel a bit anxious about how you will do in the class. You wonder if you'll be required to speak up in class, and you experience just a small amount of fear about this. When this happens, allow your muscles to relax, say something to yourself like, "I'll just allow my muscles to loosen." Now begin imagining that calm scene. Allow yourself to visualize it until you physically feel more relaxed. Try a counter or two. For example, "I'm sure there will be other people there who will also be a little anxious . . . I'm not alone."

It is important that you realize that these techniques are intended to be progressive in nature. The more you practice using them, the more helpful they will become. In fact, some psychologists call these techniques, "progressive relaxation," indicating that you gradually improve with practice, and that you should start using them in low anxiety-producing situations (like the example above) and move gradually towards using them in situations producing greater amounts of anxiety.

Desensitization

Now you are ready to employ an effective technique called desensitization. Think about some type of activity that arouses irrational thoughts and anxious feelings inside you. It could be that you feel anxious whenever:

  you speak in front of a group
  you take a test or exam
  you are out on a date

you are asked to pray in a group
you speak to your boss
you fly in an airplane
you are around horses
you are at a social gathering
someone criticizes you
someone compliments you
a woman begins talking with you
you have a lot of work to be done in a short amount of time
a job interview is approaching
you're cooking for company, wondering how the food will turn out
you wonder about making "ends meet" and how the check book will balance
your children are in competition with other children (academically, socially, athletically).

If you'd like to decrease your worry and anxiety about one of these or some other fear, first make a list of several little scenes which are related to your fear and anxiety. For example, if you are anxious at social gatherings you might come up with a list such as this:

1. Sitting at home thinking about a party coming up three days from now.
2. Seeing the word "party" in print, while you're reading a book.
3. Watching people interact at a social gathering on T.V.
4. Talking with one other person.
5. Sitting with two other people you don't know very well, in your own house.
6. Asking someone else a question at a small social gathering.

7. Answering someone else's question at a party where two other people are listening in.
8. Driving to a party where there will be a large number of people.
9. Walking into a room where there are ten other people whom you don't know very well.
10. Introducing yourself to someone at a party.

Now rank order the list of scenes from the least fearful to the most. Make sure that you have as many scenes that produce lower amounts of anxiety as you do scenes which produce high amounts. The ideal would be for each of your ten scenes to be ranked, so that scene #2 would produce just a bit more fear than scene #1, scene #3 just a bit more than scenes #1 or #2, etc. Just be sure that your selections are specific situations which could occur in the future.

Now begin relaxing in a quiet place where you won't be interrupted. Use the "muscle relaxation" and "visual imagery" techniques to allow yourself to relax. Relax for about two or three minutes. When you feel relaxed, begin imagining the first scene on your list—the one which produces the least amount of anxiety. Picture every detail. Experience it for about 20 seconds. Don't let your mind wander. Stick with that scene for the entire 20 seconds. Now turn that scene off. Turn it off completely. Return to your "calm scene" which you used during your visual imagery portion of relaxation. Just keep switching back and forth, ten or twelve times, between your anxiety producing scene and your calm scene. You should begin to feel the tension in your "tense" scene gradually going down.

Now take scene #2 on your list and repeat the same cycle. Continue on to scene #3. Switch back and forth between your "calm scene" and "tense scene" #3 until you feel the tension going down as you imagine #3. Stop. The next day, practice again, beginning with scene #3 and moving through scenes #4, #5, and #6. Continue on up your hierarchy of fearful situations until you've reached scene #10 and can feel relaxed while imagining this scene. You should now feel less anxiety when actually approaching the real situations related to the fear you've been working on.

If you have trouble getting through one of your steps and are still experiencing a lot of anxiety with it after 10 or 12 times, pick a new scene for that step. Make your new scene such that it produces a bit more anxiety than the earlier scene, yet not as much anxiety as the scene you've thrown out. Then try the difficult scene again. It is important that you make each step gradual in your hierarchy or list. In other words, don't jump from a scene that produces a little anxiety right into the next step which produces large amounts. Small steps are the key.

Meditation

I have found a simple little meditation technique to be a helpful way for me to "take a 10 minute vacation" in the middle of the day. I simply sit alone in my office and begin to relax. I begin imagining a calm scene, saying things to myself like, "My hands are warm" or "my stomach is quiet and relaxed," about 10 or 12 times each. Then I begin to chant to myself, "the peace of God . . . the peace of God . . . the peace of God." I do this very slowly and effortlessly about 10 to 20 times, with my eyes closed. Then I merely concentrate on the "peace of God." If another thought interrupts, I momentarily allow this and then again go back to concentrating and meditating on God's peace. Ten minutes later I feel as if I'd had 10 minutes of real communion with my Maker. I really do feel at peace—at one with my Lord. I feel refreshed and alive, ready to continue with the day.

Telling Yourself To Relax

While you are practicing your relaxation exercises you can say words to yourself like, "calm," "tranquil," "serene," or "peaceful," Make sure you do this from time to time. Then eventually when you are experiencing some fear or anxiety in a real-life situation, just repeating some of these words several times will have a relaxing, tranquilizing affect on you. Remember to be gentle with yourself as you silently say these words. You use these words in just the opposite manner in which you use counters. You don't shout "relax" to yourself. Instead you very easily and gently offer this word. You suggest it to yourself, slowly and effortlessly.

Other Relaxation Strategies

Once you have mastered the above pro-cedures, try some of these:

1. Begin to relax with your eyes open. Practice this by gradually opening your eyes while relaxing to mood music.
2. Next learn to relax in the same way while watching T.V.
3. While walking down the street relax your face muscles, neck and shoulders, stomach, back and chest. This will teach you to remain partially relaxed while being active.
4. Place note cards in strategic places which give you a cue to relax. For example, one woman placed a sign "SLOW DOWN " near her telephone to remind her to practice speaking in a well modulated voice. Another person placed a sign on the dash board of his car which stated "TAKE IT EASY."
5. Use humor. John Shelton, a counseling psychologist, suggests an interesting technique to decrease anxiety. Since it is impossible to be amused and anxious at the same time, he described the following concerning Ellen, one of his clients. "Ellen Z was an attractive twenty-three-year old buyer for a women's fashion store who became moderately uncomfortable at the thought of airplane travel. Since her problem was not considered incapacitating, a relatively simple treatment plan proved effective. Ellen experienced immense relief from anxiety by imagining humorous scenes while engaged in activities which triggered anxiety. For example, immediately prior to an airplane trip to Chicago, she happened to see a fifty-year-old woman complete with potbelly

and stumpy legs dressed in a miniskirt and gold knee boots. By imagining this comical sight whenever some aspect of the air travel made her anxious, Ellen was able to enjoy her flight in relative comfort."[3]

Thank God for the psychological research which gives us some of these strategies. Thank God for His word and His continual presence with us. There is perhaps no passage of Scripture which better paints a picture of God's care for us than:

Because the Lord is my Shepherd,
I have everything I need!
He lets me rest in the meadow grass
and leads me beside the quiet streams. He restores my failing health. He helps me do what honors him the most.
Even when walking through the dark
valley of death I will not be afraid, for you are close beside me, guarding, guiding—all the way.
You provide delicious food for me in
the presence of my enemies. You have welcomed me as your guest; blessings overflow!
Your goodness and unfailing kindness
shall be with me all of my life, and afterwards I will live with you forever in your home. (Psalms 23 TLB)

1. Adapted from *The Edge of Adventure: Response Manual,* Keith Miller and Bruce Larson (Waco, Texas: Creative Resources, 1974), p. 78.
2. Adapted from *Help Yourself: A Guide to Self-Change.*
3. John Shelton and Mark Ackerman, *Homework in Counseling and Psychotherapy* (Springfield, Illinois: Charles Thomas 1974).

8

Dealing With Depression

❧━━◦✣◦━━❧

Depression is a pervasive problem in our country. One out of every eight persons can be expected to require treatment for depression in their lifetime. Even though there are no simple solutions, there are some strategies for coping with feelings of depression.

What is Depression?

Perhaps the quickest way to understand what depression looks like is to describe its presence in another person. Several Biblical characters experienced depression firsthand. One of them was Moses. Several times while leading the Israelites in the wilderness, Moses became discouraged. The people were constantly complaining about how awful things were in this new "Promised Land" and how they wished Moses had never led them out of Egypt. In Numbers 11: 11-15 we hear Moses describe his feelings of depression: "Moses said to the Lord, 'Why pick on me, to give me the burden of a people like this? Are they my children? Am I their father? Is that why you have given me the job of nursing them along like babies until we get to the land you promised their ancestors? Where am I supposed to get meat for all these people? For they weep to me saying, 'Give us meat!' I can't carry this nation by myself! The load is far too heavy! If you are going to treat me like this, please kill me right now; it will be a kindness! Let me out of this impossible situation!" (TLB)

What was Moses experiencing? For one thing, he had lost hope. He felt he could not go on. He'd rather die than have to put forth any more effort. He was in despair. Second, he had lost his perspective. He was not thinking clearly because he couldn't see the forest for the trees. He could not figure out any possible solutions. Third, he had a strong desire to escape and withdraw from life. He cried, "Let me out of this impossible situation!" Fourth, he was angry at both God and the Israelites. We can hear his anger in statements like, "Where am I supposed to get meat for all these people?" and "I can't carry this nation all by myself!" Fifth, he was feeling very dependent. He wanted someone else to come up with the answers. Most of Moses statements in this passage were in the form of questions put to God about how to go on with the everyday tasks of his life. And sixth, he was feeling inferior. This is seen in the last sentences.

Notice how God deals with Moses. In verses 16 and 17 the Lord says, "Summon before me seventy of the leaders of Israel; bring them to the Tabernacle, to stand there with you . . . they shall bear the burden of the people along with you, so that you will not have the task alone." God was saying to Moses, "Look, what you often do is attempt to do everything yourself. Then, after awhile, the burden becomes too heavy because you haven't delegated out responsibility to some of the other leaders. Go easier on yourself. Ask for help when you need it. It's a good way to prevent depression and despair. Allow others to stand with you in all of this."

Again, in Exodus 18:12-22 Moses attempts to carry all of the burdens of the people on his own shoulders. This time Moses' father-in-law gives him some of the same sound advice: "Why are you trying to do all this alone . . . It's not right! . . . You're going to wear yourself out—and if you do what will happen to the people? Moses, this job is too heavy a burden for you to try to handle all by yourself. Now listen, and let me give you a word of advice, and God will bless you." if you read the rest of the verses in this passage you will see how Moses' father-in-law advises Moses to delegate responsibility in order to share the burden of his work with others. In this ancient passage of Scripture we have a modern principle of management and healthy psychological functioning which I share in counseling with every single depressed person I meet. "Share your burdens with others. Ask for what you need. Don't go through life without the support of friends who care!" In my opinion, many persons could substantially decrease their feelings of depression through following this principle alone.

Another common reason for depression is guilt. In Psalm 51 we have the dramatic feelings of guilt which David felt at one time. Nathan, the prophet had just come to inform David of God's judgment on him because he had committed adultery with Bathsheba, and because he had Uriah, her husband murdered. Here are some of David's feelings: "O Loving and kind God, have mercy. Have pity upon me and take away the awful stain of my transgressions. Oh, Wash me, cleanse me from this guilt. Let me be pure again. For I admit my shameful deed—it haunts me day and night!" (TLB) David was down! He was consumed with guilt. And his guilt was real. He had done some pretty bad stuff. But in this Psalm, he works out this guilt by expressing his broken spirit, remorse and penitence to God. Here is a model of what we are to do with guilt. We are to confess it to our Lord, with a broken and contrite heart. He will surely forgive us!

If you are feeling an overwhelming sense of guilt, please share this openly. Here are several steps you can take: One, express the depths of your remorse to God, in prayer. Two, go to a pastor who believes in the value of confession and will hold your expressed guilt in confidence. Again pour out your feelings of guilt to that person. Have the pastor pray with you concerning your misdeeds. The importance of accepting forgiveness on faith and thanking the Lord for that forgiveness can not be overemphasized. Three, after you have confessed, take the step of faith and thank Christ Jesus for His forgiveness. Take a deep breath of air and let it out. As you let go of that breath of air, also let go of your guilt. If you have any recurrence of these guilt feelings, simply say silently, "Thank you Jesus, You have forgiven me" and then go on about whatever you are doing. Use this phrase as a counter to your nagging irrational doubts that God has forgiven you. In God's Word we have many assurances that we are forgiven our shortcomings. Luke 5:20 states, "Your sins are forgiven." (TLB) Romans 4:6-8 implies that our sins are "put out of sight," (TLB) when we confess them in faith. Romans 5:8 says that we are "loved by God even while we were still sinners." (TLB) Other passages which you may find helpful include:

Romans 8:1
I Corinthians 6:9-11
Ephesians 1-4
Colossians 1:14
Colossians 1:22
I Peter 1:3
I John 2:12

From Elijah, the prophet, we learn still more about depression, its causes and how it can be prevented. You can read, in detail, about his life as it relates to depression in I Kings 18 and 19. Let me highlight parts of this for you. Beginning in I Kings 18:41, we have the beginning of an account which probably contributed to Elijah's later despondency. First he climbed up Mt. Carmel during mealtime. Then he climbed back down the mountain and raced, on foot, for twenty miles, ahead of the king's chariot. Then Jezebel threatened his life. He was scared, physically exhausted, hungry, and probably dwelled considerable on the threat to his life. He believed that everyone, including God, had deserted Him. Then he did a peculiar thing. Instead of gathering friends around him, of which he had many, we are told in I Kings 19:4 (TLB) that "he went on *alone* into the wilderness, traveling all day (becoming still more exhausted), and sat down under a broom bush and prayed that he might die. 'I've had enough,' he told the Lord, 'take away my life. I've got to die sometime, and it might as well be now.'" Elijah had experienced several causes of depression:

> Insufficient rest
> Physical exhaustion
> Poor food intake
> Isolated himself from friends
> Irrational, negative thinking
> Self-pity

He had brought them on himself.

How did God deal with him in order to lift the depression? He did not criticize Elijah for his depression. He certainly did not tell Elijah that being depressed was sinful. Instead, he sent an angel to minister to Elijah. The prophet slept and was given food. He was encouraged by God to talk about his depression. The prophet opened up, telling God of his concerns and worries. Then God did a couple things. In verse 18 He reminded Elijah of his faulty thinking about how many friends he had: "And incidentally, there are 7000 men in Israel who have never bowed to Baal nor kissed him!" God also urged Elijah to get into action (to counteract his apathy and despair). He was giving Elijah the realistic hope that he could actually do something about his depression. And, with God's help, he did.

Grief Depression, Experiencing a Loss

A common cause of depression is through the experience of a loss. This could be the death of a spouse, divorce, marital separation, loss of hand or leg, a son or daughter leaving home, moving from one community to another, loss of a job, or any number of other real or perceived loss of someone or something. Many people, when they experience sad feelings around these times, tend to deny them. We are told to be brave. "Keep a stiff upper lip. Don't get upset. It does no good to cry. It must have been God's will." I'm sure we've all heard each one of these accolades. Maybe we've even given a few now and then, basically because we were afraid of the real feelings that lay just underneath that "stiff upper lip."

What we need to do when we have sad feelings is to express them. We need to share these feelings openly with someone we are close to and can trust. For me, it is most helpful if that person is a ready listener who will take the time and effort required to really tune into my sadness. I need someone who will hold off on advice-giving unless I ask for it.

I have seen many people experience grief in several different forms. Losses which are the most traumatic (such as death of a loved one, divorce, etc.) tend to take around two years before the person is ready to move on and really begin living again. This is a normal time frame for such an adjustment. However, when these sad feelings are held in and seldom, if ever expressed, those persons often take much longer to work through such losses. These individuals tend to become quite depressed and disillusioned with life. When you experience a loss, you need to "talk it out" with "ready listeners."

Causes of Depression

From the discussion above I've pointed out several causes of depression. I'd like to list them briefly, along with several others, because overcoming depression can only be accomplished if we understand its causes.

1. *Experiencing a loss.* The depression from such an event can be heightened if the feelings of remorse are repressed. Express these feelings!

2. *Poor diet.* When persons become depressed they often have little or no appetite. Poor eating habits during this time will only add to the depression. So eat regular, nutritious meals. Force yourself to do this when you are feeling blue. You may have to eat five or six times a day and consume smaller amounts. That's okay. The important thing is to eat good food.

3. *Not enough sleep or rest.* Recently I counseled with a young man whose wife was having an affair. Instead of lying down and at least resting at night, he would go chasing all over the city in his automobile, trying to catch his mate in the act. The result was, that he did not get any sleep. After a week of this kind of behavior, he had become so depressed that he had to begin taking anti-depressants in order to keep suicidal

thoughts from getting the best of him. I strongly urged him to at least stay home nights and rest even though he could not sleep. After two or three nights of bed rest, his depression lifted to the point where he no longer needed the anti-depressants.

4. *Anger that is repressed.* If you are the type of person who seldom expresses any anger to anyone, you are a good candidate for depression. For the feeling of depression can be the result of unexpressed anger that is turned inward, upon yourself. I am not suggesting, here, that you should become an old grouch, continually dumping your rage on everyone in sight. What I'd like to suggest is that, for starters, you re-read the two chapters on "Speaking The Truth In Love."

5. *Reaction to drugs.* Reactions to certain drugs can affect a person's moods. Medications administered to correct a physical disturbance may cause a chemical change in the body that brings on the blues. All drugs affect the body and the mental processes in some way. If a drug results in brain or nervous system toxicity, extreme depression could be the result. If a person takes too much of a drug or sedative over an extended period of time, he may become a candidate for toxic depression. The symptoms are listlessness, indifference, and difficulty in concentrating. Often the person evidences odd and illogical thought patterns which interfere with his normally good judgment. In many cases the depression and drug toxicity will clear up in a day or so after the drug is no longer in the

system.[1]   If you are taking any kind of medication and become depressed, you should seek your physician's advice immediately.

6. *Physical causes.* Hypoglycemia (low blood sugar), infections of the brain or nervous system, general body infections, hepatitis, hormonal irregularities, and either a low or hyperthyroid condition can all cause depression. Again, the point here is to see a physician if you're depressed, even if you're involved in counseling for the depression.

7. *Physical exhaustion.* Remember Elijah?

8. *Guilt.* I've already described some strategies for dealing with guilt in this chapter.

9. *Faulty thought life.* Perhaps you're talking yourself into depression. For some useful strategies see the chapter on "Your Thought Life."

Moving Away From Helplessness

Here are some additional "helps" that have been useful in my own counseling practice with depressed persons.

1. *Preplan your daily activities.* When you are "down" it is often very difficult to get up and get going in the morning. You feel very much like just lying there and letting the world go by. If this happens to you, I encourage you to *preplan, the night before, on paper,* all the things you will do the next day. If you have a spouse or close friend who will help you with this by gently, yet firmly encouraging you, ask their help.

2. *Get out of bed immediately upon awakening.* I

have found that many people tend to lie in bed in the morning and talk themselves into a depression. They say to themselves, "Oh, how I dread this day. I just know it will be even worse than yesterday. I just can't face another day at work. I'll never make it through this week!" By the time that person gets up, feelings of depression have set in, and a dreary tone for the day has been set. My advice, if this is the case with you, is to do the following upon awakening. Say to yourself, "This is the day the Lord has made. I will rejoice and be glad in it!" Then arise immediately! Jog, or get involved in some type of exercise for 5 to 10 minutes. Then hit the shower. Adjust it to warm and move in. Scrub yourself briskly and feel the sensations. Begin to adjust the water to cooler and cooler positions until you can no longer tolerate it. Then jump out. Dry yourself briskly. Talk to your room-mate, spouse, or call a friend as soon as possible. Refer to your activity list which you've prepared the night before. Begin planning in your mind for the first activity on the list. This sets the stage for a better day than if you had remained in bed groveling in negative thoughts. Congratulate yourself at this point! Praise the Lord!

3. *Use your counters!* A negative thought life, as I've discussed in Chapter 6, can raise havoc with your spirits. Attack those thoughts that just don't hold water. For example, if you feel that your boss is really displeased with your work, check it out with that person. You may be right, but you could also be wrong. Remember, if

you make an assumption always put that assumption "on trial." Verify it, and see if it is true. If you discover that a particular thought is untrue, write down the reasons why it is false. Say these reasons out loud. Thank God for helping you find out that these negative thoughts are false and unproductive. Learn to say to yourself, "I'm jumping to conclusions again," or "I blew things all out of proportion again." Some other counters that are sometimes helpful with depression, are:

"I'm catastrophizing again!"
"Give yourself a break!"
"I'd better check out the facts."
"I assumed that she didn't like it, but it could be just as possible that she did like it."

4. *Give yourself directions.* Remember this strategy from Chapter 6? You merely come up with little phrases which trigger you to engage in constructive actions. For depression some of these phrases might be:

"Get out of bed and start moving!"
"Call a friend!" "Talk to someone who will listen."
"Exercise today!"
"Get out of the house!"
"Focus on some positive stuff!"
"Get some rest."
"Eat something, even if it's a small portion."

H. Norman Wright, in *Training Christians To Counsel* suggests that initially, when you become depressed, you use the following directions:

> For now, say this to yourself: "Okay, I am depressed. There are reasons why I'm depressed, and they are valid reasons.
>
> "My depression is telling me that something is bothering me about the way I am living my life. While it is very painful, it may help me to understand myself better."
>
> When you feel down on yourself, tell yourself, "I'm going to learn something from this experience. And I am going to feel better." Say this to yourself as many times a day as you need to. [2]

The reason you can follow these directions with some confidence is that the statements made are largely true. There are usually some valid reasons why you are blue. Once you sort out these reasons, you may discover some of them to be irrational. But for the moment, in your experience, they are valid. It is also true that we often learn something about ourselves through negative experiences. Finally, it is true that even severe depressions usually end.

As you use some of these directions and counters write them on cards. Post them in strategic spots around your house or apartment. When you are feeling down, it is difficult to cue yourself on your own. These external reminders can be very helpful.

5. *Use of Scripture.* There are several passages you may find meaningful, when you are blue:

Philippians 4:6-9
Psalm 147:3
Psalm 42:11
Isaiah 41:10
Psalm 43:5
Psalms 40:1, 2
Luke 4:18

Use the thought-stopping technique, discussed in Chapter 7. Remember to write the word STOP! on one side of the note card and your scripture on the other side.

Memorize several of these passages, saying them to yourself periodically during the day. In Ephesians 4:23 we are reminded that this is good practice: "And be constantly renewed in the spirit of your mind—having a fresh mental and spiritual attitude." (Amplified) And II Timothy 3:16 couldn't state more clearly how powerful God's word really is: "The whole Bible was given to us by inspiration from God and is useful to teach us what is true and to make us realize what is wrong in our lives; it straightens us out and helps us do what is right." (TLB)

6. *Other Books*. Several books I have read which are useful in understanding and overcoming depression are:

1. Cammer, Leonard. *Up From Depression.* Pocket Books, Inc., New York, N.Y., 1969.

2. De Rosis, Helen and Victoria Pellegrino. *The Book of Hope: How Women Can Overcome Depression.* Macmillan Publishing Co., New York, N.Y., 1976.

3. Hauck, Paul A. . *Overcoming Depression.* Westminster Press, Philadelphia, Pa., 1973.
4. Wright, Norman. *An Answer to Depression.* Harvest House Publishers, Irvine, Ca., 1976.

7. Be a plodder. Whenever I feel that little, if anything is going right, I plod along. By that I mean that I force myself to go ahead and do some of the insignificant things that need to get done and that I've put off. This may involve writing letters, making contacts, setting up appointments, writing out bills, fixing something or working with my hands in some other way, shopping for essentials, or making phone calls. Anything that results in some concrete finished product or goal which I can "check off" on a list is good. This gets me involved in some type of activity, so that I don't spend all of my time sitting catastrophizing about how horrible things are.

8. *Scan your environment for positive things.* For five minutes out of each hour, stop what you are doing and tune in to all the positive, good things that are going on around you. Take note of pleasant physical surroundings, people you like, pleasant smells, colors, and sounds. Focus on these positive aspects of your present moment, weeding out and blocking any negative thoughts or sensations. Then say, "Thank you, Lord, for my blessings!"

9. *Get out of the house.* Even if it's for short periods of time leave the house several times per day. You could walk to a nearby store or pay a

neighbor a brief visit. Go to a place you enjoy. Take a walk.

10. *See people you know and like.* Push yourself to see friends and family members often. You may want to see them for only short periods of time; but that's okay. If there are things that people close to you are doing which are not helpful, tell them. For example, sometimes others try to joke with us when we're depressed. Or they may criticize or scold us. Tell them that what you *do need* is support, warmth, empathy and gentle firmness and encouragement.

11. *Have one or two persons you can really unload to.* This is someone whom you can trust, someone who will listen even to your anger and your complaints about life.

12. *Eat.* Even if this means eating several very small meals or snacks in a day. Often when people are depressed they cannot eat very much food at one sitting. So go ahead and snack five or six times a day, *if you have this trouble.* If you *overeat* when you're depressed, don't take this suggestions as an excuse to increase your problem!

13. *See a physician.* If your depression continues for over a week see your family doctor for a check-up. Tell the doctor about your depression and ask him if there's any physical basis for it.

14. *See a counselor.* Thank God some of our stigmas about seeing a counselor are breaking down. Preferably select a professional who is at least sympathetic to your religious feelings, and

is not bent upon attacking your beliefs on the grounds that they are Christian and therefore, irrational and supposedly at the heart of your problem.

1. H. Norman Wright, *The Christian Use of Emotional Power*. (Old Tappan, N.J.: Fleming H. Revell, 1974), p. 78.
2. H. Norman Wright. *Training Christians to Counsel*. (Denver: Christian Marriage Enrichment, 1977), p. 78.

9

Enriching Your Marriage Relationship

❦❧

*"We walk among worlds unrealized until we have
learned the secret of love."*   —Hugh Black

According to John Gottman, a professor of
psychology at the University of Illinois, the most
consistent research finding about what is
different in the communications of strangers
and people married to each other is that
married people are ruder to each other than
they are to strangers. They interrupt their
spouses more, put their spouses down more,
hurt each other's feelings more, and are less
complimentary to each other. [1]

Marital disharmony is a major social problem.
Approximately one out of three married couples
are unhappy with their marriage. This unhap-
piness is not something which necessarily
passes with time. The longer one is married, the
greater is the probability of dissatisfaction.
Termination of unhappy marriages by divorce is
on the increase, as is the number of children in
the disrupted marriages. Crime and delinquency
is greater for children who are products of

unhappy or broken homes. Alcoholism is more frequent among the separated. About one-half of first admissions to state mental hospitals result from marital stresses as the single major precipitating condition! Since 95 percent or more of the adult population has at least one marriage in a lifetime, marital disharmony is a pervasive social problem.

The Three Stages of Marriage

In my own counseling I have observed couples in three general stages or "passages" in their relationship. These stages are not always clear-cut, and from month to month a couple might waver back and forth among all three stages. However, marriage generally proceeds through the following "passages:"

Stage I-The Happy Honeymoon

When you begin your love relationship you tend to feel good about everything. You do not want that special feeling to go away, so you tend to avoid conflict. If your partner does something that annoys you, you ignore this because you don't wish to rock the boat or take the risk of losing that beautiful feeling of being in love.

Each of you probably focuses on the other's merits, disregarding any defects. There is, most likely, a tendency to put each other on somewhat of a pedestal. "She has such a great personality" (ignoring the fact that at times you are annoyed with her incessant talking). Or "He is so calm about everything" (when you have sometimes wondered if he ever talks about any feelings).

In this stage there is often a tendency to express love by giving. One partner may cook delicious meals that are pleasing to the other. Another partner may bring home flowers or write poetry and love notes. There is also an inclination to "give-in" during a potential conflict. If one wishes to go to a movie and the other wants to eat out, they may fall over each other trying to compromise. During this time there is also an inexhaustible interest shown in each other's feelings. Both tend to be really tuned in to each other's needs. There is also a tendency toward supporting each other, no matter what the difficulty or trouble might be.

Again, highly threatening problems are avoided because it feels so good to be close. In this way topic after topic, which the couple ought to be talking about, is shoved underneath the carpet, only to surface at times of crises later in the relationship, or when it may be too late.

This stage does leave the couple with a sense of how they can have fun and enjoy each other. It also introduces them to some areas they will later have to really work on, such as:

1. Being complimentary toward each other, focusing on each other's merits, as opposed to spotlighting negative attributes.
2. Really tuning in to each other's feelings.
3. Expressing love through giving to the other. Doing special things for your partner.
4. Supporting each other.
5. Developing a variety of ways to share fun

and enjoyment together—just the two of you.

Near the end of this stage, real-world obligations begin to pile up. Children may come. The couple may buy a house and assume a large mortgage. One or both partners may be striving diligently to launch a career, leaving less time for the relationship. During this time of added stress, evidence of each other's shortcomings begins to pile up. Perhaps that woman with the great personality has suddenly turned into a constant "motor mouth." Or that strong silent type has now become a "non-communicator" who "never tells me his feelings." This marks the beginning of a period of mutual disillusionment.

Stage II—Mutual Disillusionment

After 5-8 years of marriage the honeymoon stage is usually passed. The disillusionment near the end of Stage I continues, along with disappointment and regrets concerning the selection of the partner. "How did I miss all of this while we were dating!" may be the retort often heard. Or "You're not the same girl I married. What's happened to you?" What's happened is that perhaps the couple was not completely honest with each other during that Honeymoon Stage, and now the truth is coming out at last. "You never take my feelings into account. I always have to do everything your way, and I'm sick and tired of it!" The baffled spouse might say, "Well you never told me that all of this is bothering you. How could I know?" The snappy comeback may sound like this: "You should just know what I'm feeling! You sure used to when we were dating."

Once these kind of battles begin it's very difficult to get out of them. Each partner begins to use their spouses' weaknesses against them. "You're just like your mother. You have no mind of your own." Or "You and your dad are identical, no guts, no backbone, no nothing!" This kind of communication closes us up. It keeps couples from really sharing with each other for the fear of being bruised by thoughtless words. And so, instead of learning what and how to communicate effectively during this stage, we often learn what *not* to talk about. And tragically these are the very things which the couple *must* talk about in order to keep their marriage together.

There is an extreme contrast between the acceptance of each other during Stage I and the present rejection that continually occurs in Stage II. There is an extreme disappointment in oneself. And with this comes a drop in self-esteem. "I'm a real nag!" might be a continual part of ones thought-life. Or "I'm just a plain failure as a father. I'm never with my kids because I work all of the time. I never take my wife anywhere! I'm just not cut out for marriage!"

There is also a tendency to point the old finger at your partner and say, in effect, "You're responsible for all of this mess, in fact, you're responsible for my bad feelings. If you didn't nag all of the time . . . If you'd be home more . . . If only you'd shut up and listen to me . . . If only you'd think about something other than sex . . . If you'd fix yourself up I just might give you some attention . . . " So there is a mutual kind of blame.

And there is a mutual kind of withholding of self. To guard ourselves from being hurt during this stage, we cut ourselves off emotionally from our partners. We give very little emotionally to each other. And because we are not getting much we are not about to give much. And the more wronged we feel the more ruthless we become in our put-downs and rejection. And love dies slowly, unless we do something about it. For this is the stage of hard work. We simply must work on our relationship, at this stage, in order to move back in the direction of mutual support and caring.

Norman Wright in a helpful book entitled *The Fulfilled Marriage* states very succinctly what we need to realize in Stage II:

> "Love is more than a feeling. Love is a commitment to an imperfect person. When we have this attitude a new sense of realism enters the marriage and makes growth possible.[2]

In this stage we need to realize that love is an inner commitment; it is knowing that you love even when you don't *feel* it. To love somebody is not just a strong feeling—it is a decision, it is a judgment, it is a promise.[3] There may be times when you have little or no feeling, but you still know that you love the other person. And this love can be deepened and enhanced emotionally by the way you act toward your spouse. Edward Ford said, "It is in the very process of doing things with and for others that you begin to fall in love. It is in the very process of doing things with and for others that you stay in love."[4]

What is needed at this stage is a re-visitation of the positive things you experienced in Stage I. You need to listen to one another again in a caring, supportive way. What has happened to those warm glances across a room, that wink, that warm touch, that compliment which used to come so easily? Start in again doing these things, even if they feel awkward at first. You're only out of practice. You were able to respond in this way at one time, so you can probably do it again. Make a list of the things you know your partner would enjoy. Put them into practice by doing one of them per day during the next week. At a recent seminar Joyce Landorf suggested that each spouse in the room make a list of ten things they could do or say that would indicate to their partners that they loved them. Then she urged everyone to "act out" one of those ways of showing love to our partners each day for the rest of our lives. Try it, your partner will love it!

Stage III—Reaching for Harmony

If persons are able to work through their conflicts and differences in Stage II, there is added hope they will move into Stage III. During this time there is a growing confidence that the relationship will last. It has stood the test of several crises and there is a sense of peace and harmony along with a belief or trust in the strength of the relationship. There are still conflicts and disagreements, but there is also the living out of Ephesians 4:2: "Be patient with each other, making allowance for each other's faults because of your love." (TLB) This dealing with conflict in "patience and making allowances" is not done in the same "phony" way in which it was done in Stage I. There is now a healthy combination of leveling with each other and yet being polite while locating the issues that threaten to disturb the relationship. Ephesians 4:26 says it well, "If you are angry, don't sin by nursing your grudge . . . " In the same verse we are told, "Don't let the sun go down with you still angry—get over it quickly . . ." (TLB) In other words, it's okay to feel the emotion of anger, and it is okay to express it. In fact we are instructed to express anger soon after we feel it. It's how that anger is expressed to one another that makes the difference. We are neither to withhold all our anger, nor are we to blast away at will, calling our partners names and "hitting below the belt" with cheap, destructive words.

Stage III couples have arrived here through hard work in Stage II. They have come to this place, not by pointing their fingers at each other, nor by wallowing in self-indignation and pity. They have brought their relationship back into relative harmony by each examining their own behavior and changing what needed to be changed.

These couples also tend not to put everything into that one relationship. Both partners have recognized the need for outside relationships with other friends. To put your burden for happiness completely upon the marital relationship is simply demanding too much of it. Each of us needs other interests and other people to share them with. In this way we develop our own selves separate from our partners and bring newness of life back into the marriage. One way to test this out in your own marriage would be to sit down together and conduct a conversation in which you can talk about anything except work and children. If your conversation gets nowhere at that point you'd better talk about developing some outside interests that you can either develop on your own or together.

In this final stage there is also a mutual acceptance of one another. There is a feeling that the family is becoming a safety valve where you express yourself like nowhere else. There is also a kind of mutual accommodation or helping each other out instead of blaming the other or "pointing the old finger." This is the kind of marriage where each partner seeks out the other for pleasure and fun. There are several common interests they share. Finally these couples find that their relationship is one of the most productive ways of being able to risk and grow by then returning to a secure, lasting intimacy with each other.[5]

ENRICHING YOUR OWN MARRIAGE
Faultfinding—the key to failure

Karen and I have always felt that we had a good, solid marriage. And that has really been true over our 10 years together. However, a couple of years ago at a marriage enrichment weekend we re-discovered a concept that has enhanced our marriage ever since. The concept is this: FAULTFINDING IS BASICALLY DE- STRUCTIVE TO A RELATIONSHIP. The first half day of this weekend was structured to be an encounter with self. We were told to ask ourselves questions like:

1. Write a one minute description of yourself.
2. What are my good points?
3. What are my bad points?
4. What are my masks, my facades?
5. Do I really like myself?
6. What negative symptoms are presently existing in our marriage?
7. What do I feel I can do to eliminate these symptoms?

That was a tough time, looking at ourselves. It was a time of recognizing that "pointing the old finger" was not the way to improve our marriage. Rather a more constructive way was to ask regarding question number seven, "What can I do to eliminate these symptoms?"

You see, continual faultfinding is destructive because it in effect is saying, "I do not accept you as a less than perfect human being." When faultfinding is the basic way of communicating, a home becomes a place of misery and hostility. Continual criticism only serves to store up resentment. The fact is, faultfinding is one of the poorest methods known for changing the behavior of others. The person who is locked into giving primarily negative feedback becomes an object to be feared or hated. Each year I see scores of marriages where resentment has built up to the point of no return, because negative feedback has become the principal way of communicating.

The book of Proverbs speaks out loud and clear on this point. "A good man things before he speaks; The evil man pours out his evil words without a thought." (Proverbs 15:28 TLB) "Self-control means controlling the tongue! A quick retort can ruin everything." (Proverbs 13:3 TLB) "Gentle words cause life and health; griping brings discouragement." (Proverbs 15:4 TLB)

"Faultfinding is a consequence of reliance on certain destructive defense mechanisms. The typical faultfinder either projects his own shortcomings onto another person or displaces his anger toward one person (e.g., boss) onto another (e.g., wife). Most often, faultfinding is an unconscious way of trying to hide one's own weaknesses by projecting them onto someone else . . ."[6]

Okay! So we're not to be faultfinders. What would be better? Here are some strategies I've both tried in my own marriage as well as in the marriage counseling I do with others:

1. *Positive Exchange.* Each of you develop a list of "Ten Things I Love About My Partner." These things should be very specific. That is, don't list "You are beautiful." That's too general. Something like "I love the way your eyes sparkle when you're pleased about something," would be better. Here are some things I've listed about Karen:

1. "I love your inner strength, your ability to bounce back in a crisis." (I gave an example.)
2. "I like your ability to listen to people and get them talking about themselves."
3. "I like the way you support me when I'm hurting."
4. "I like the little surprises you buy me or do for me."
5. "I love the way you teach our boys things. Your creativity in this regard amazes me! (I gave an example.)
6. "I think you have pretty eyes, especially with the new hairdo you have now."

Now take your lists and in a face-to-face position, with good eye contact, say (one at a time) what's on your lists to each other, slowly, and with feeling. Two rules need to be observed: One, do not turn your positives into negatives. For example, while doing this exercise one person said, "I really like your new hair style. Now all you need to do is learn how to dress!" State your compliment as a compliment, without qualifications. Two, the person receiving the compliment must look the other person in the eye and say, "Thank you." Do not give the "positive stroke" back by saying, "Oh, that really isn't true" or "I just can't believe you mean that!" Allow yourself to take in the "warm fuzzies" your partner is giving you. Enjoy them. Remember this: "It is better to light one candle, than to curse the darkness."

2. *Caring Days*. Dr. Richard Stuart, a prominent psychotherapist and author, has suggested this

very helpful method for showing your partner you love them. To employ this procedure, each of you should write down between 10 and 20 positive actions which you would like to have your partner perform toward you. These are not negative actions which you want your spouse to cease doing, but positive, loving, caring actions. Make sure that these actions are so specifically stated that by reading them your spouse will know exactly what to do. Now exchange your lists. Now, each of you, without telling the other of your plans, will select one day during the week and perform as many of these caring acts as you can during that day.[7] Do as many of these loving gestures as possible. You may end up selecting the same day and barrage each other with kindness all at once or you may choose separate days. It doesn't matter.

Why do this? For one, it opens up several different ways of showing love toward your partner. Two, Caring Days illustrate to each partner that their mate is capable of really giving in the relationship. Three, *increasing positive actions* toward each other *decreases* the number of negative actions. If you're doing loving things to each other there's less time to do the negative!

Here is a sample of one couple's list of caring behaviors which they wanted the other to perform toward them.

Sample Request List
For Caring Days

Wife's Requests
1. Tell me you love me.

2. Wink at me across a crowded room of people.
3. Go horseback riding with me.
4. Tell me when I look attractive.
5. Kiss me in the morning before you go to work.

6. Cuddle with me at night before we go to sleep, even if we aren't going to have sex.
7. Put your things away in the den when you come home from work.
8. Bring me a rose or carnation.
9. Take a shower in the evening and put on my favorite shaving lotion.
10. Look at me intently and directly sometimes when I'm telling you something.
11. Baby-sit the children while I play tennis with a friend.
12. Tell me a joke. Liven me up. Tickle me.
13. Make breakfast and serve it to me.
14. Take Robert (their son) to preschool.

Husband's Requests
1. Give me a big hug when I come home from work.
2. Call me at work.
3. Give me a back rub.
4. Tell me about your work today.
5. Sit closer to me when we are riding in the car together.
6. Hug me when we are in public.
7. Tell me that you love me.
8. Bring me a cup of coffee.
9. "Brag" about me a little in public.
10. Tell me I'm a hard worker, when you think so.

11. Go to lunch with me. (Can you imagine her turning this one down?)

Once you have done a Caring Day or Positive Exchange, don't stop at that point. To keep your giving kind of love going engage in Caring Days as often as you like during the rest of your marriage. Set a goal to give your spouse at least one compliment a day. Take one action off your partner's "Request List for Caring Days" and do it! Set another goal to honor one of these "Requests Lists," and begin again with some new ways of caring.

3. *Be Alone Together.* A few days ago a woman said to me, "I'd be afraid to be alone with my husband over a weekend. We haven't been somewhere, just the two of us, for years! I wonder if we'd have anything to talk about?" Spend some time alone together each week. That could mean going out for coffee together, lunch, for a walk, or nestled together in your family room in front of the fireplace with the kids in bed. Much of the spark of your Honeymoon State was lit while you spent solitary time with each other. That's how you really became intimate in the first place. In order to remain intimate, you still need this time alone together. Plan some ways you can accomplish this during the next week. You'll probably feel closer as a result. I recommend that all couples, in addition to the regular weekly times alone, spend at least two overnights together each year at a motel, resort, or camping.

Communicating: Listening and Talking

Too bad communicating isn't that simple: listening and talking. However, the importance of communication in marriage is shown in a study that compared happily married couples with unhappily married couples. Results indicated that those happily married:

1. talked more to each other.
2. conveyed the feeling that they understood what was being said to them.
3. had a wider range of subjects available to them to talk about.
4. preserved the communication channels and kept them open no matter what happened.
5. showed more sensitivity to each other's feelings.
6. made more use of supplementary nonverbal techniques of communication.[8]

In my own counseling office I spend 25-30 hours per week helping couples straighten out their twisted communication patterns. What are the causes of faulty communication? Books have been written on this subject alone, and my purpose is not to point so much at causes as toward solutions. Suffice it to say that when couples do not listen, do not speak directly to each other and communicate that they are listening, they get into trouble with each other emotionally. What are some possible solutions?

Listening

One of the most important, loving things you will ever do to another person is listen to them. To listen to someone is, in effect, to say, "I love you enough to believe that what you are saying is very important." By listening to our partners we become their person of choice to talk to when the chips are down or when they have something exciting to share. So many marital partners have drifted away from each other because the basic human need of being listened to and therefore prized was not being met in their own marriage relationship. The result is often an extra-marital friendship with a person of the opposite sex that becomes more important than the relationship with the spouse.

According to King James Bible, "A wise man will hear, and will increase learning . . ." (Proverbs 1:5). James 1:19 states: "Let every man be quick to hear (a ready listener) . . ." (Amplified). This same passage in The Living Bible says ". . . don't ever forget that it is best to listen much . . ."

I thank God for our five year old son, Cory. Recently I was proofreading parts of this manuscript during an evening at home. Apparently Cory had been speaking to me and I had been nodding and grunting occasionally, but not really tuning in to what he was saying. All of a sudden there was silence. Very firmly, yet gently Cory removed the manuscript from my grip. He said, "Dad I know you have to write books, but right now you need to listen to me." And he was right. We entered into a beautiful dialogue at that point. That dialogue might have been lost had Cory not reminded me he needed my undivided attention for a few moments.

What is listening? How do we go about doing it most effectively? If you want to communicate to someone that you are really tuning in to what they are saying, do the following:

1. *Face that person squarely.* This means that your body is pointed openly and directly toward the person you are listening to.

2. *Lean forward slightly.* This communicates to the person that you are trying to get into their "space" and that you want to experience part of their world.

3.*Keep good eye contact.* This does not mean staring the person down. However, if you are looking into the other person's eyes most of the time you are again communicating that you are interested and concerned.

4. *Concentrate on what the other person is saying in the here and now.* Do not be thinking about what you are going to say when the other person stops talking. If you are going to really tune in, it will take all of your energies just to stay with the person in the present.

5. *Completely accept what the other person is saying and how it is stated, without judgment.* Just as your feelings and ideas are valid for you, so are your partner's. If you find yourself strongly disagreeing with what your partner is saying, before you put in your two cents worth, be sure and validate what your spouse has said. A statement such as "I can see how being in your shoes you'd really feel that way . . . I probably would too," would communicate your empathy and non-judgmental attitude. This point is critical! Validating and accepting another person's experience as real and

legitimate for them is half the battle in good marital communication. You greatly increase your chances of being heard by your spouse if you first *hear* what your spouse is saying and communicate acceptance of what you are hearing. This does not mean that you must agree with your spouse. It means you communicate that what your partner is experiencing is valid for them.

6. *Restate accurately both the content and feeling of a message.* Periodically make statements like, "Now I want to be sure that I'm catching all that you're saying. Let me know if this is it . . . " Then summarize what you heard your partner saying. If you have caught the essence of what's been said, your spouse will let you know. And if you haven't, let your partner repeat the message until you can accurately restate what has been conveyed to the other person's satisfaction. When you summarize use different words and phrases than were originally used by your spouse. This will make your response less redundant and more natural.

Talking To Your Partner

Ephesians 4:31-32 states clearly what we should be striving for in human relationships: "Stop being mean, bad-tempered, and angry. Quarreling, harsh words, and dislike of others should have no place in your lives. Instead, be kind to each other, tenderhearted, forgiving one another . . . "(TLB) Yet it seems as though the easiest thing to do in close personal relationships is to show the worst side of our nasty selves. There are several things we do which circumvent kindness, tenderheartedness and forgiveness. Some of the more prevalent include:

1. *Giving out contradictory messages.* Saying "How was your day?" while you walk into another room. Or, the husband, leaving for work says, "I really love you, honey!" But after he has left his wife has to pick up several things he has left lying all over the house.

2. *Using shut-offs.* Uttering words like, "Shut up!" or "Yeah, yeah!" Walking to another room. Hiding behind a newspaper. What kind of shut-offs do you use in your marriage?

3. *Using volatile words.* "*All* men are like that!" "*Nothing* comes out right for me!" "You *always* do that!" "You *never* do anything right!" One of the first rules I try to get couples to abide by in marriage counseling is to *not* use the words *never, always, nothing,* and *all.* These words are an invitation to fight. Most sentences directed at your partner containing these words are irrational statements which simply don't hold water. Monitor your own use of these volatile words during some week in the future. Get a rough estimate on how often you use them and then attempt to decrease their frequency in the ensuing week. Begin to substitute words such as "sometimes," "frequently," "at times," in the same kind of statements and notice the result. Your spouse will more often hear what you're saying because your statements will be more near the truth. "*Some* men are like that." "*At times* things don't go right for me." "You do that *frequently.*"

4. *Assuming others share your feelings.* One of the most difficult tasks to do with our spouses is to allow them their own feelings. We often make statements like, "How can you feel that way?" or "How can you like that?" or "Why didn't you do it the right way?" (my way). Each of us has our own separate identities, values, etc. and to deny each other those rights is to breed hostility. Again, good validation, restating and summarizing content and feelings you hear your spouse saying are key.

5. *Mind Reading.* When one partner is relatively non-communicative and the other is more extraverted, there is a tendency for the more outgoing partner to attempt mind reading. "I just know you're not *really* feeling good about that." or "I'll bet you're just boiling inside, or maybe you're sad . . . glad? . . . confused?" There's no quicker way to turn off a non-communicator than through interpreting and mind reading. Let your spouse speak for himself. Back off and say something like, "I feel as though you'd like to talk more about this and I want you to know that when you're ready to talk about it I'll be here, ready to listen." Then back off.

6. *Getting "Off Beam."* You just began a fairly straightforward discussion about how to handle the finances in your relationship. All of a sudden you are fighting about something completely off the subject. You're "off beam" and someone needs to say, "we got off track here, I'd like to get back to what we were originally talking about." Many unresolved issues stay unresolved

in marriage because of not sticking to the issue which needs to be discussed. Unresolved issues tend to produce tension and anger in relationships.

7. *Cross-complaining.* This happens when each spouse states a complaint in response to a complaint. For example:

Wife: "I really wish we could go out more."

Husband: "What do you think I'm made of money? All you want to do is spend money!"

Wife: "Look whose talking about money! I suppose your new little Honda was a cheap item! We could have gone out every night for a year on what it cost you to buy that thing!"

Husband: "Oh, all you know how to do is nag, nag, nag!"

What can be done to get yourselves out of this pattern? For one, you can validate each others' point of view:

Wife: "I really wish we could go out more."

Husband: "I can sure understand your dilemma. You're home with the kids most of the time and I'm out and away from home all day." AND THEN ADD ONE OF THE MOST POWERFUL STATEMENTS YOU CAN MAKE IN A MARRIAGE RELATIONSHIP: *"What can we do to make things better?"* Now you're ready to solve the problem. And your spouse no longer has to say to herself, "If only he could see all the stress that I'm going through and see all that I've done for him and us." And if you're asked the question, "What can we do to make things better?" a good way to respond is, "Well, here is one thing I'd be willing to do in order to make things better."

The next step could be for both of you to brainstorm as many possible solutions to the problem as you can. This involves merely getting out as many ideas as you can without anyone criticizing those ideas. Then you could mutually select the most workable solutions.

Do *not* state complaints in negative or ambiguous ways, such as:

> "You're never affectionate!" or
> "You're inconsiderate!"

Instead state complaints in positive, specific terms:

> "I would appreciate it if you would touch and hug me more often."
> "I'd like you to ask me how my day was, when you come home from work."
> "I would like to have you pay me compliments."

The requests above tell the spouse exactly what you'd like. They are not put-downs, as most negatively stated complaints tend to be. Complaints stated in the form of positive specific requests, greatly increase the chances of some positive response on the part of your partner.

Rules for Communication

Some rules that I've found helpful to couples in my own marriage counseling include:

1. *Do not dig up the negative past.* Especially in arguments or disagreements, stay with the present issue. Don't dig back any further than 3 months ago. In Philippians 3:13 the Apostle Paul says it well: "No, dear brothers, I am still not all

I should be but I am bringing all my energies to bear on this one thing: Forgetting the past and looking forward to what lies ahead . . . '' (TLB)

2. *Decide what you will talk about.* For example, you may agree to respect each other's political views and not argue about them.

3. *Decide when you will talk.* You may decide that it is best not to begin discussing disagreements until both of you have been home from work for at least one hour. Or it may be that the best time to resolve conflicts is late at night, because you're both "night owls."

4. *Decide on the duration of conversation.* It may be that four hour discussions tend to turn into "all out brawls" or that these long conversations tend to get you down. Perhaps you can agree that all "heavy" discussions be limited to one hour.

In closing I'd like to share with you a very meaningful statement about marriage that was handed to me last year by a young woman after I had delivered a talk on Marriage Enrichment to a group of preschool parents. In beautiful language it summarizes several of the points I've made in this chapter.

OUR MARRIAGE CREED

COMFORT EACH OTHER . . . Provide a refuge and sanctuary for each other from the chill winds of the world. Your marriage is a hearth, from whence comes the peace, harmony, and warmth of soul and spirit.

CARESS AS YOU WOULD BE CARESSED . . .
Warm your loved one's body with your heal-
ing touch. Remember that as babies can die
with lack of touching, so can marriages wit-
her from lack of closeness.

BE A FRIEND AND PARTNER . . . Friendship can
be a peaceful island, separate and apart, in a
world of turmoil and strife. Reflect upon the
tranquility of the many future years you can
share with a true friend and beware of becoming enemies under the same roof.

BE OPEN WITH EACH OTHER . . . Bind not yourselves in the secretness that causes suspicion
and doubt. Trust and reveal yourselves to
each other, even as the budding rose opens to
reveal its fragrance and beauty.

LISTEN TO EACH OTHER . . . And hear not only
words, but also the non-language of tone,
mood, and expressions. Learn to listen to
understand rather than listening to argue.

RESPECT EACH OTHER'S RIGHTS . . . Remember that each is a person of flesh and blood,
entitled to his or her own choices and mistakes. Each owns himself, and has the right to
equality.

ALLOW THE OTHER TO BE AN INDIVIDUAL . . .
Seek not to create for each other a new mold
that can only fit with much discomfort and
pain. Accept the other as they are, as you
would have yourself accepted.

GIVE EACH OTHER APPROVAL . . . Remember criticism divides, while compliments encourage confidence in the other. Hasten not to point out the other's mistakes, for each will soon discover his own.

CHERISH YOUR UNION . . . Let no one come between your togetherness, not child, not friend, nor worldly goods. Yet maintain enough separateness to allow each other his or her own unique oneness.

LOVE ONE ANOTHER . . . Love is your river of life—your eternal source of recreating yourselves. Above all else—love one another.

1. John Gottman, et. al. *A Couple's Guide To Communication.* (Champaign, Illinois: Research Press, 1976).
2. Norman Wright, *The Fulfilled Marriage.* (Irvine, California: Harvest House, 1976).
3. Erich Fromm. *The Art of Loving,* (New York: Harper & Row, 1956), p. 56.
4. Edward Ford. *Why Marriage?* (Niles, Illinois: Argus, 1974), p. 58.
5. Adapted from Goldstine, D., Larner, K., Zuckerman, S. and Goldstine, H. *The Dance Away Lover.* (William Morrow, 1977).
6. Steven Wahlroos. *Family Communication* (New York: Macmillan, 1974), pp. 20-21.
7. Richard Stuart, "An Operant Interpersonal Program for Couples," in *Treating Relationships* by David Olson (Graphic Publishing, 1976), p. 119.
8. C. Broderick, ed., *A Decade of Family Research and Action.* (National Council on Family Relations, 1970), p. 67.

NOTES:

NOTES:

NOTES: